BEYOND THE POST-MODERN MIND

BEYOND THE
POST-MODERN MIND

HUSTON SMITH

CROSSROAD · NEW YORK

1982
The Crossroad Publishing Company
575 Lexington Avenue, New York, NY 10022

Library of Congress Cataloging in Publication Data

Smith, Huston.
  Beyond the post-modern mind.

  1. Philosophy, Modern—20th century—Addresses,
essays, lectures. I. Title.
B804.S576   190'.9'04   81-17475
ISBN 0-8245-0457-7   AACR2

For Serena, Sierra, and Tony
and the future they stand for

CONTENTS

Acknowledgments

Had it not been for the initiative of Richard Payne of The Crossroad Publishing Company and his consultant, Ewert Cousins, these essays would not have been assembled. Had not Douglas Sloan, editor of the *Teachers College Record* requested "Excluded Knowledge," and he and the Charles F. Kettering Foundation commissioned "Beyond the Modern Western Mind-set," those essays would not have been written. My graduate assistants, William Cuozzi, Anne Bevan-Wilson, M. L. Vogel, Carl Lindquist, and Jonathan Rosenbloom have researched a number of facts. Students at Syracuse University, especially those in its Graduate Program in Religion, have been stimulating, and my colleagues in religion and philosophy have provided high-spirited criticism and basic support. My wife Kendra's editorial eye improves with each successive book. A grant from the Senate Research Committee of Syracuse University underwrote preparation of the final typescript. Don and Joan Miller provided an ideal hideout for correcting proofs and preparing the index.

To all of these, my sincerest thanks.

Preface

"If, by some strange device, a man of our century could step backwards in time and mix with the people of a distant age," Gai Eaton wrote in *The King of the Castle,* "he would have good cause to doubt either their sanity or his own" (p. 7). The sun's daily cycle, a raven's flight, mossy oaks and water gushing from a glade would look familiar enough, but the meanings they carried for his new associates would be different. Each would think he knew what constitutes common sense and human normality, but their common sense would differ from his and their normality might seem to him abnormal. Questioning everything they took for granted and astonished that they did not see how much their conclusions were controlled by arbitrary assumptions, he would find everything he took for granted similarly called into question. His "Why?" would be met with their "Why?", and he would have no answer.

The essays here assembled attempt a move like the one just envisioned: they invite us to step outside our current Western outlook to see it in perspective. The limitations of earlier outlooks are so obvious that we forget that ours, too, is built on premises history will smile on. Science and the historical record we now possess may seem to exempt us from the perspectival character of human vision, but we know, of course, that they do not. Like those who have lived before us, we too have fished certain objectives from the sea of human possibilities. These in turn have firmed up premises that support them, and from these premises an entire outlook has been spun—all this these essays try to show. To compare our world view with others is not to set light against shadow. It is to compare twilight zones; different kinds of limitations, "as though a man tunneling his way out of prison were to emerge within the perimeter, exchanging one cell for another. So it must always be," Eaton concludes, "unless the prisoner learns that freedom lies in quite another direction, never through the tunnel of time" (ibid.).

We shall encounter this other, atemporal and non-cumulative dimension of knowledge in the third essay of this book, but here the point is that on the temporal continuum peoples' outlooks pass through discernible stages, and the one the West has occupied in this century I have called the Post-Modern Mind to distinguish it from the Modern Mind which has come to be associated with the seventeenth-through-nineteenth century outlook. Everyone who has given the slightest thought to epistemology and the sociology of knowledge concedes the point that has been made thus far—that this mind (like others) is limited—but in the West almost everyone assumes that it is less limited than the ones that preceded it. That presumption, too, these essays challenge. At most we have achieved a trade-off, exchanging depth for breadth; but even that assertion is generous, for depth is more important *than* breadth. It is as if, standing before a picture window that opens onto an alpine landscape, we have lowered the shade to the point where we can now see little more than the ground at our feet. True, science has empowered us to see that ground in ways that are awesome in themselves, but it is still not the Matterhorn. On page 76 below we shall find *The Chronicle of Higher Education* reporting that "if anything characterizes 'modernity' it is a loss of faith in transcendence," and if we add that the loss is incalculable and unnecessary, we have the thesis of this book. The Post-Modern Mind is not the ample, roomy mind we suppose. Against the horizons of human thought that part two sketches, it is seen for what it is: misshapen in being dwarfed and flat.

Alternatively in these pages the Post-Modern Mind is characterized as shapeless. Flat and shapeless are incompatible, but in this case both pertain as applying to part and whole. As a whole, the Post-Modern Mind lacks form and definition, but a part of that mind—its cutting edge, one might say, as represented by the university and reflective minds outside it—has contours that are well defined. We see these most clearly when we notice what they rule out and delegitimize, and my fourth essay, "Excluded Knowledge," uses this criterion to bring them to sharp focus. When speaking specifically of this cutting edge of the Post-Modern Mind, I use the designation Modern Western Mind-set. Its clear boundaries never extend to the Post-Modern Mind as a whole because it can say almost nothing about values and existential meanings (see pp. 66–67 and 111–12 below). This leaves people to fend for themselves in these important areas, with the resulting pluralism one would expect.

The essays in part one describe the Post-Modern Mind in its inclusive, enveloping formlessness. Part three narrows attention to the cutting edge of that mind, the Modern Western Mind-set. For the outlines of this latter to be brought to clear focus, a stable reference point is needed, and part two establishes it. Part four looks toward release from the strictures of the Modern Western Mind-set which are becoming daily more apparent.

To try to step outside the perspective of one's own culture is a little like trying to step out of the shoes one is walking in. My talents for the move are no greater than the next man's, but circumstances have been in my favor. Born and raised in a foreign and traditional society, China, the longest stretch of my career was at the Massachusetts Institute of Technology, a spearhead of the modern, Western, scientific age. Two worlds were thereby joined. If the slant of these essays seems surprising at any point, the reason may derive from that intersection.

Two "housekeeping" details:

In a collection of essays that deal with a common theme but were written for different audiences, a certain amount of overlap is inevitable. By editing I have reduced this somewhat, but have not tried to eliminate it entirely, hoping that what remains can serve a constructive purpose. When the reader comes to a point that is being repeated, he can be sure that it is crucial for the book's argument. Seen in this way, the restatements can be taken as opportunities for review—occasions to make sure that the point is firmly in mind before proceeding.

In this awkward time respecting genders, I have not tried to be consistent in my use of them. To write "he or she" every time would be cumbersome, but occasionally I gesture in that direction to acknowledge that a problem exists; one that I hope will eventually be resolved.

Part One

DARK WOOD

Of the two senses in which the Post-Modern Mind is used in this book—to refer to the current Western ethos as a whole and to its most reflective cutting edge—I begin with the first. If we include persons from all walks of life and the numberless directions in which their hopes and thoughts extend, we can only conclude what has become a truism: that no comprehensive vision, no concerted sense of reality, informs our age. The opening lines of Dante's *Divine Comedy* could have been written for our twentieth-century's Everyman:

> *Midway this way of life we're bound upon*
> *I woke to find myself in a dark wood,*
> *Where the right road was wholly lost and gone.*

Near the century's start, John Dewey pointed to "despair of any integrated outlook and attitude [as] the chief intellectual characteristic of the present age," and every succeeding decade has borne him out. Heidegger believed that ages are powered by works of art that gather scattered practices into unified, persuasive models for behavior, and hold them before people who can then relate to each other along the lines they exemplify. Our age, though, he felt, is the first whose paradigm is a work, not of art but of technology: the hydroelectric power station. Being a technological construct, it is value-free. The power station converts the river's power into a grid that places it at the disposal of any purpose whatever. As electricity can be used to satisfy any desire we happen to have, this paradigm provides no directives or motivation for action at all. The consequence is a vacuum of meaning and purpose, as Saul Bellow, too, noted in his 1976 Nobel Laureate Lecture:

> The intelligent public is waiting to hear from Art what it does not hear from Theology, Philosophy, Social Theory, and what it cannot hear from pure science: a broader, fuller, more coherent, more comprehensive account of what we human beings are, who we are, and what this life is for. If writers do not come into the center it will not be because the center is preempted. It is not.

I used an invitation from *The Saturday Evening Post* to contribute to its "Adventures of the Mind" series as occasion to look at this empty center.

$$\cdot 1 \cdot$$

THE REVOLUTION
IN WESTERN THOUGHT*

Quietly, irrevocably, something enormous has happened to Western man. His outlook on life and the world has changed so radically that in the perspective of history the twentieth century is likely to rank—with the fourth century, which witnessed the triumph of Christianity, and the seventeenth, which signaled the dawn of modern science—as one of the very few that have instigated genuinely new epochs in human thought. In this change, which is still in process, we of the current generation are playing a crucial but as yet not widely recognized part.

The dominant assumptions of an age color the thoughts, beliefs, expectations, and images of the men and women who live within it. Being always with us, these assumptions usually pass unnoticed— like the pair of glasses which, because they are so often on the wearer's nose, simply stop being observed. But this doesn't mean they have no effect. Ultimately, assumptions which underlie our outlooks on life refract the world in ways that condition our art and our institutions: the kinds of homes we live in, our sense of right and wrong, our criteria of success, what we conceive our duty to be, what we think it means to be a man or woman, how we worship our God or whether, indeed, we have a God to worship.

Thus far the odyssey of Western man has carried him through three great configurations of such basic assumptions. The first constituted the Graeco-Roman, or classical, outlook, which flourished up to the fourth century A.D. With the triumph of Christianity in the

* Reprinted with permission and negligible changes from *The Saturday Evening Post*, 26 August 1961.

Roman Empire, this Graeco-Roman outlook was replaced by the Christian world view which proceeded to dominate Europe until the seventeenth century. The rise of modern science inaugurated a third important way of looking at things, a way that has come to be capsuled in the phrase "the Modern Mind."

It now appears that this modern outlook, too, has run its course and is being replaced by what, in the absence of a more descriptive term, is being called simply the Post-Modern Mind. What follows is an attempt to describe this most recent sea change in Western thought. I shall begin by bringing the Christian and modern outlooks into focus; for only so can we see how and to what extent our emerging thought patterns differ from those that have directly preceded them.

From the fourth-century triumph of Christianity in the Roman Empire through the Middle Ages and the Reformation, the Western mind was above all else theistic. "God, God, God; nothing but God"—in the twentieth century one can assume such an exclamation to have come, as it did, from a theologian. In the Middle Ages it could have come from anyone. Virtually without question all life and nature were assumed to be under the surveillance of a personal God whose intentions toward man were perfect and whose power to implement these intentions was unlimited.

In such a world, life was transparently meaningful. But although men understood the purpose of their lives, it does not follow that they understood, or even presumed to be capable of understanding, the dynamics of the natural world. The Bible never expands the doctrine of creation into a cosmogony for the excellent reason that it asserts the universe to be at every point the direct product of a will whose ways are not man's ways. God says, "Let there be"—and there is. That is all. Serene in a blaze of lasting light, God comprehends nature's ways, but man sees only its surface.

Christian man lived in the world as a child lives in his father's house, accepting its construction and economics unprobed. "Can anyone understand the thunderings of God's pavilion?" Elihu asks Job. "Do you know the ordinances of the heavens, how the clouds are balanced or the lightning shines? Have you comprehended the expanse of the earth, or on what its bases were sunk when the morning stars sang together and all the sons of God shouted for joy?" To such rhetorical questions the answer seemed obvious. The leviathan of nature was not to be drawn from the great sea of mystery by the fishhook of man's paltry mind.

Not until the high Middle Ages was a Christian cosmology attempted, and then through Greek rather than Biblical inspiration, following the rediscovery of Aristotle's Physics and Metaphysics. Meanwhile nature's obscurity posed no major problem; for as the cosmos was in good hands, it could be counted on to furnish a reliable context in which man might work out his salvation. The way to this salvation lay not through ordering nature to man's purposes but through aligning man's purposes to God's. And for this objective, information was at hand. As surely as God had kept the secrets of nature to himself, he had, through his divine Word and the teachings of his church, made man's duty clear. Those who hearkened to this duty would reap an eternal reward, but those who refused to do so would perish.

We can summarize the chief assumptions underlying the Christian outlook by saying they held that reality is focused in a person, that the mechanics of the physical world exceed our comprehension, and that the way to our salvation lies not in conquering nature but in following the commandments which God has revealed to us.

It was the second of these three assumptions—that the dynamics of nature exceed man's comprehension—which the sixteenth and seventeenth centuries began to question, thereby heralding the transition from the Christian to the modern outlook. The Renaissance interest in the early Greeks revived the Hellenic interest in nature. For the first time in nearly two thousand years Western man began to look intently at his environment instead of beyond it. Leonardo da Vinci is symbolic. His anatomical studies and drawings in general disclose a direction of interest that has turned eye into camera, in his case an extraordinary camera that "could stop the hawk in flight and fix the rearing horse." Once again man was attending to nature's details as a potential messenger of meaning. The rage to know God's handiwork was rivaling the rage to know God himself.

The consequence, as we know, was modern science. Under scrutiny, nature's blur was found to be provisional rather than final. With patience the structure of the universe could be brought into marvelous focus. Newton's exclamation caught the excitement perfectly: "O God, I think thy thoughts after thee!" Although nature's marvels were infinitely greater than had been supposed, man's mind was equal to them. The universe was a coherent, law-abiding system. It was intelligible!

It was not long before this discovery began to reap practical rewards. Drudgery could be relieved, health improved, goods multiplied and leisure extended. As these benefits are considerable, working with intelligible nature began to overshadow obedience to God's will as a means to human fulfillment. God was not entirely eclipsed—that would have entailed a break with the past more violent than history allows. Rather, God was eased toward thought's periphery. Not atheism but deism, the notion that God created the world but left it to run according to its own inbuilt laws, was the Modern Mind's distinctive religious stance. God stood behind nature as its creator, but it was through nature that his ways and will were to be known.

Like the Christian outlook, the modern outlook can be sum- ✗ marized by identifying its three controlling presuppositions. First, that reality may be personal is less certain and less important than that it is ordered. Second, man's reason is capable of discerning this order as it manifests itself in the laws of nature. Third, the path to human fulfillment consists primarily in discovering these laws, utilizing them where this is possible and complying with them where it is not.

The reason for suspecting that this modern outlook has had its day and is yielding to a third great mutation in Western thought is that reflective men are no longer confident of any of these three postulates. The first two are the ones that concern us here. Frontier thinkers are no longer sure that reality is ordered and orderly. If it is, they are not sure that man's mind is capable of grasping its order. Combining the two doubts, we can define the Post-Modern Mind as one which, having lost the conviction that reality is personal, has come to question whether it is ordered in a way that man's reason can lay bare.

It was science which induced our forefathers to think of reality as primarily ordered rather than personal. But contemporary science has crashed through the cosmology which the seventeenth-to-nineteenth-century scientists constructed as if through a sound barrier, leaving us without replacement. It is tempting to attribute this lack to the fact that evidence is pouring in faster than we can throw it into perspective. Although this is part of the problem, another part runs deeper. Basically, the absence of a new cosmology is due to the fact that physics has cut away so radically from our capacity to imagine the way things are that we do not see how the two can get back together.

If modern physics showed us a world at odds with our senses, post-modern physics is showing us one which is at odds with our imagination, where imagination is taken as imagery. We have made peace with the first of these oddities. That the table which appears motionless is in fact incredibly "alive" with electrons circling their nuclei a million billion times per second; that the chair which feels so secure beneath us is actually a near vacuum—such facts, while certainly very strange, posed no permanent problem for man's sense of order. To accommodate them, all that was necessary was to replace the earlier picture of a gross and ponderous world with a subtle world in which all was sprightly dance and airy whirl.

But the problems the new physics poses for man's sense of order cannot be resolved by refinements in scale. Instead they appear to point to a radical disjunction between the way things behave and every possible way in which we might try to visualize them. How, for example, are we to picture an electron traveling two or more different routes through space concurrently or passing from orbit to orbit without traversing the space between them at all? What kind of model can we construct of a space that is finite yet unbounded, or of light which is both wave and particle? It is such enigmas which have caused physicists like P. W. Bridgman of Harvard to suggest that "the structure of nature may eventually be such that our processes of thought do not correspond to it sufficiently to permit us to think about it at all. . . . The world fades out and eludes us. . . . We are confronted with something truly ineffable. We have reached the limit of the vision of the great pioneers of science, the vision, namely, that we live in a sympathetic world in that it is comprehensible by our minds."

This subdued and problematic stance of science toward reality is paralleled in philosophy. No one who works in philosophy today can fail to realize that the sense of the cosmos has been shaken by an encyclopedic skepticism. The clearest evidence of this is the collapse of what historically has been philosophy's central discipline: objective metaphysics, the attempt to discover what reality consists of and the most general principles which describe the way its parts are related. In this respect, the late Alfred North Whitehead marked the end of an era. His *Process and Reality: An Essay in Cosmology* is the last important attempt to construct a logical, coherent scheme of ideas that would blueprint the universe. The trend throughout the twentieth century has been away from faith in the feasibility of such undertakings. As a tendency throughout philosophy as a whole, this is a revolutionary development. For twenty-five hundred years philosophers have argued over which metaphysical system is true. For them to agree that none is, is a new departure.

The agreement represents the confluence of several philosophical streams. On one hand, it has come from the positivists who, convinced that truth comes only from science, have challenged the metaphysician's claim to extrascientific sources of insight. Their successors are the linguistic analysts, who have dominated British philosophy for the last several decades and who (insofar as they follow their pioneering genius Ludwig Wittgenstein) regard all philosophical perplexities as generated by slovenly use of language. For the analysts, "reality" and "being in general" are notions too thin and vapid to reward analysis. As a leading American proponent of this position, Professor Morton White of Harvard recently stated, "It took philosophers a long time to realize that the number of interesting things that one can say about all things in one fell swoop is very limited. Through the effort to become supremely general, you lapse into emptiness."

Equal but quite different objections to metaphysics have come from the existentialists who have dominated twentieth-century European philosophy. Heirs of Kierkegaard, Nietzsche, and Dostoevski, these philosophers have been concerned to remind their colleagues of what it means to be a human being. When we are thus reminded, they say, we see that to be human precludes in principle the kind of objective and impartial overview of things—the view of things as they are in themselves, apart from our differing perspectives—that metaphysics has always sought. To be human is to be finite, conditioned, and unique. No two persons have had their lives shaped by the same concatenation of genetic, cultural, historical, and interpersonal forces. Either these variables are inconsequential—but if we say this we are forgetting again what it means to be human, for our humanity is in fact overwhelmingly shaped by them—or the hope of rising to a God's-eye view of reality is misguided in principle.

The traditional philosopher might protest that in seeking such an overview he never expected perfection, but that we ought to try to make our perspectives as objective as possible. Such a response would only lead the existentialist to press his point deeper; for his contention is not just that objectivity is impossible but that it runs so counter to our nature—to what it means to be human—that every step in its direction is a step away from our humanity. (We are speaking here of objectivity as it pertains to our lives as wholes, not to restricted spheres of endeavor within them such as science. In these latter areas objectivity can be an unqualified virtue.) If the journey held hope that in ceasing to be human we might become gods, there could be no objection. But as this is impossible, ceasing to be human can only mean becoming less than human—inhuman in the usual sense of the word. It means forfeiting through inattention the birthright that is ours: the opportunity to plumb the depths and implications of what it means to have an outlook on life which in important respects is unique and will never be duplicated.

Despite the existentialist's sharp rebuke to metaphysics and traditional philosophy in general, there is at least one important point at which he respects their aims. He agrees that it is important to transcend what is accidental and ephemeral in our outlooks and in his own way joins his colleagues of the past in attempting to do so. But the existentialist's way toward this goal does not consist in trying to climb out of his skin in order to rise to Olympian heights from which things can be seen with complete objectivity and detachment. Rather it consists in centering on his own inwardness until he finds within it what he is compelled to accept and can never get away from. In this way he, too, arrives at what he judges to be necessary and eternal. But necessary and eternal for him. What is necessary and eternal for everyone is so impossible for a man to know that he wastes time making the attempt.

With this last insistence the existentialist establishes contact with the metaphysical skepticism of his analytic colleagues across the English Channel. Existentialism (and its frequent but not invariable partner, phenomenology) and analytic philosophy are the two dominant movements in twentieth-century philosophy. In temperament, interest, and method they stand at opposite poles of the philosophical spectrum. They are, in fact, opposites in every sense but one. Both are creatures of the Post-Modern Mind, the mind which doubts that reality has an absolute order which man's understanding can comprehend.

Turning from philosophy to theology, we recall that the Modern Mind did not rule out the possibility of God; it merely referred the question to its highest court of appeal—namely, reality's pattern as disclosed by reason. If the world order entails the notions of providence and a creator, God exists; otherwise not. This approach made the attempt to prove God's existence through reason and nature the major theological thrust of the modern period. "Let us," wrote Bishop Joseph Butler in his famous *The Analogy of Religion,* "compare the known constitution and course of things . . . with what religion teaches us to believe and expect; and see whether they are not analogous and of a piece. . . . It will, I think be found that they are very much so." An enterprising Franciscan named Ramon Lull went even further. He invented a kind of primitive computer which, with the turning of cranks, pulling of levers, and revolving of wheels, would sort the theological subjects and predicates fed into it in such a way as to demonstrate the truths of the Trinity and the Incarnation by force of sheer logic working on self-evident propositions. Rationalism had entered theology as early as the Middle Ages, but as long as the Christian outlook prevailed, final confidence was reserved for the direct pronouncements of God himself as given in Scripture. In the modern period, God's existence came to stand or fall on whether reason, surveying the order of nature, endorsed it. It was as if Christendom and God himself awaited the verdict of science and the philosophers.

This hardly describes the current theological situation. Scientists and philosophers have ceased to issue pronouncements of any sort about ultimates. Post-modern theology builds on its own foundations. Instead of attempting to justify faith by appeals to the objective world, it points out that as such appeals indicate nothing about reality one way or the other, the way is wide open for free decision—or what Kierkegaard called the leap of faith. One hears little these days of the proofs for the existence of God which seemed so important to the modern world. Instead one hears repeated insistence that however admirably reason is fitted to deal with life's practical problems, it can only end with a confession of ignorance when confronted with questions of ultimate concern. In the famous dictum of Karl Barth, who has influenced twentieth-century theology more than anyone else, there is no straight line from the mind of man to God. "What we say breaks apart constantly . . . producing paradoxes which are held together in seeming unity only by agile and arduous running to and fro on our part." From our own shores Reinhold Niebuhr echoed this conviction. "Life is full of contradictions and incongruities. We live our lives in various realms of meaning which do not cohere rationally."

Instead of "These are the compelling reasons, grounded in the nature of things, why you should believe in God," the approach of the church to the world today tends to be, "This community of faith invites you to share in its venture of trust and commitment." The stance is most evident in Protestant and Orthodox Christianity and Judaism, but even Roman Catholic thought, notwithstanding the powerful rationalism it took over from the Greeks, has not remained untouched by the post-modern perspective. It has become more attentive to the extent to which personal and subjective factors provide the disposition to faith without which theological arguments prove nothing.

It is difficult to assess the mood which accompanies this theological revolution. On one hand, there seems to be a heightened sense of faith's precariousness: as Jesus walked on the water, so must the contemporary man of faith walk on the sea of nothingness, confident even in the absence of rational supports. But vigor is present too. Having labored in the shadow of rationalism during the modern period, contemporary theology is capitalizing on its restored autonomy. Compensating for loss of rational proofs for God's existence have come two gains. One is new realization of the validity of Pascal's "reasons of the heart" as distinct from those of the mind. The other is a recovery of the awe without which religion, as distinct from ethical philosophy piously expressed, is probably impossible. By including God within a closed system of rational explanation, modernism lost sight of the endless qualitative distinction between God and man. Post-modern theology has reinstated this distinction with great force. If God exists, the fact that our minds cannot begin to comprehend his nature makes it necessary for us to acknowledge that he is Wholly Other.

These revolutions in science, philosophy and theology have not left the arts unaffected. The worlds of the major twentieth-century artists are many and varied, but none resembles the eighteenth-century world where mysteries seemed to be clearing by the hour. The twentieth-century worlds defy lucid and coherent exegesis. Paradoxical, devoid of sense, they are worlds into which protagonists are thrown without trace as to why—the world which the late French novelist Albert Camus proclaimed "absurd," which for his compatriot Jean-Paul Sartre was "too much," and for the Irish dramatist Samuel Beckett is a "void" in which men wait out their lives for what-they-know-not that never comes. Heroes driven by a veritable obsession to find out where they are and what their responsibility is seldom succeed. Most of Franz Kafka is ambiguous, but his parable, "Before the Law," closes with as clear a countermand to the modern vision of an ordered reality as can be imagined. "The world-order is based on a lie."

Objective morality has gone the way of cosmic order. Even where it has not been moralistic, most Western art of the past has been created against the backdrop of a frame of objective values which the artist shared. As our century has progressed, it has become increasingly difficult to find such a framework standing back of the arts.

A single example will illustrate the point. One searches in vain for an artistic frame of reference prior to the twentieth century in which matricide might be regarded as a moral act. Yet in Sartre's play *The Flies,* it is the first authentic deed the protagonist Orestes performs. Whereas his previous actions have been detached, unthinking, or in conformity with the habit patterns that surround him, this one is freely chosen in the light of full self-consciousness and acceptance of its consequences. As such, it is the first act which is genuinely his. "I have done my deed, Electra," he exults, adding "and that deed was good." Being his, the deed supplies his life with the identity which until then it had lacked. From that moment forward, Orestes ceases to be a free-floating form; his acquisition of a past he can never escape roots his life into reality. Note the extent to which this analysis relativizes the moral standard. No act is right or wrong in itself. Everything depends on its relation to the agent, whether it is chosen freely and with full acceptance of its consequences or is done abstractedly, in imitation of the acts of others, or in self-deception.

We move beyond morality into art proper when we note that the traditional distinction between the sublime and the banal, too, has blurred. As long as reality was conceived as a great chain of being—a hierarchy of worth descending from God as its crown through angels, men, animals, and plants to inanimate objects at the base—it could be reasonably argued that great art should attend to great subjects: scenes from the Gospels, major battles, or distinguished lords and ladies. With cubism and surrealism, the distinction between trivial and important disappears. Alarm clocks, driftwood, pieces of broken glass become appropriate subjects for the most monumental paintings. In Samuel Beckett and the contemporary French antinovelists, the most mundane items—miscellaneous contents of a pocket, a wastebasket, the random excursions of a runaway dog—are treated with the same care as love, duty, or the question of human destiny.

One is tempted to push the question a final step and ask whether the dissolution of cosmic order, moral order, and the hierarchic order of subject matter is reflected in the very forms of contemporary art. Critic Russel Nye thinks that at least as far as the twentieth-century novel is concerned, the answer is yes. "If there is a discernible trend in the form of the modern novel," he writes, "it is toward the concept of the novel as a series of moments, rather than as a planned progression of events or incidents, moving toward a defined terminal end. Recent novelists tend to explore rather than arrange or synthesize their materials; often their arrangement is random rather than sequential. In the older tradition, a novel was a formal structure composed of actions and reactions which were finished by the end of the story, which did have an end. The modern novel often has no such finality." Aaron Copland characterizes the music of our young composers as a disrelation of unrelated tones. Notes are strewn about like membra disjecta; there is an end to continuity in the old sense and an end of thematic relationships."

When Nietzsche's eyesight became too poor to read books, he began at last to read himself. The act was prophetic of the century that has followed. As reality has blurred, the gaze of post-modern man has turned increasingly upon himself.

Anthropological philosophy has replaced metaphysics. In the wake of Kierkegaard and Nietzsche, attention has turned from objective reality to the individual human personality struggling for self-realization. "Being" remains interesting only as it relates to man. As its order, if it has one, is unknown to us, being cannot be described as it is in itself; but if it is believed to be mysteriously wonderful, as some existentialists think, we should remain open to it. If it is the blind, meaningless enemy, as others suspect, we should maintain our freedom against it.

Even theology, for all its renewed theocentrism, keeps one eye steadily on man, as when the German theologian Rudoph Bultmann relates faith to the achievement of authentic selfhood. It is in art, however, that the shift from outer to inner has been most evident. If the twentieth century began by abolishing the distinction between sublime and banal subject matter, it has gone on to dispense with subject matter altogether. Although the tide may have begun to turn, the purest art is still widely felt to be entirely abstract and free of pictorial representation. It is as if the artist had taken the scientist seriously and responded, "If what I see as nature doesn't represent the way things really are, why should I credit this appearance with its former importance. Better to turn to what I am sure of: my own intuitions and the purely formal values inherent in the relations of colors, shapes and masses."

I have argued that the distinctive feature of the contemporary mind as evidenced by frontier thinking in science, philosophy, theology, and the arts is its acceptance of reality as unordered in any objective way that man's mind can discern. This acceptance separates the Post-Modern Mind from both the Modern Mind, which assumed that reality is objectively ordered, and the Christian mind, which assumed it to be regulated by an inscrutable but beneficent will.

It remains only to add my personal suspicion that the change from the vision of reality as ordered to unordered has brought Western man to as sharp a fork in history as he has faced. Either it is possible for man to live indefinitely with his world out of focus or it is not. I suspect that it is not, that a will-to-order and orientation is rather fundamental in the human makeup. If so, the post-modern period, like all the intellectual epochs that preceded it, will turn out to be a transition to a still different perspective.

·2·

THE DEATH AND
REBIRTH OF METAPHYSICS*

The preceding essay mentions Whitehead as one philosopher who tried to construct a twentieth-century cosmology, and in my graduate days at the University of Chicago his leading disciple, Charles Hartshorne, was one of my mentors. So when a 1964 *Festchrift* was published in his honor, I used my entry to commend, in effect, Whitehead's metaphysical courage. In more focused philosophical terms this time, I tried to spell out my reasons for thinking that comprehensive vision, an overview of some sort, remains a human requirement; reflective creatures cannot retain the sense of direction life requires without it. Because it is the one slightly technical essay in this collection, the general reader may wish to skip over it.

The subtitle of Charles Hartshorne's latest book sets the direction for my remarks. Titled *The Logic of Perfection,* the book is subtitled "Essays in Neo-Classical Metaphysics." Each ingredient in this characterization is pertinent. In declaring the book to be a metaphysical treatise the author dissociates himself from the positivistic suspicion that such inquiries are misguided in principle and cognitively can come to nothing. The qualification "classical," in turn, distinguishes the inquiry from dominant continental quests—Heidegger's, Jaspers's, Sartre's, Marcel's—which, though engrossed with the problem of being, doubt that traditional tools (objective reason directed toward system construction) can effectively come to grips with it. There remains the prefix "neo-," which

* Reprinted with permission from Wm. R. Reese and Eugene Freeman, eds., *Process and Divinity: The Hartshorne Festschrift* (La Salle, Ill: Open Court Publishing Co., 1964).

announces that we cannot perpetuate the past. In method as well as in content, twentieth-century metaphysics must break new ground.

Why? Necessarily? How? Fusing these questions, I wish to ask what has come over metaphysics in our time and what may be the discipline's future.

I

Deeply embedded in the history of Western civilization is a body of knowledge, conceived by the pre-Socratics, midwifed by Socrates, and born well formed in the writings of Plato and Aristotle, whose name is metaphysics. The principles that have governed its growth have been abstractness, system, and scope. Scope signifies that it has taken all things—the total range of what is—as in some sense its province; system, that it has sought to make the categories of its "scheme of things entire" hang together. Abstractness has been, simply, the inevitable price of generality: the more items you want your concepts to cover, the more the features that individualize them must be ignored. Two standard definitions summarize these traits as well as any: "Metaphysics is the endeavour to frame a coherent, logical, necessary system of general ideas in terms of which every element of our experience can be interpreted" (Whitehead).[1] "Metaphysics is concerned to reveal just that set of major classifications of phenomena, and just those precise criteria of valid understanding, by which the whole array of given experience may be set in order and each item (ideally) assigned its intelligible and unambiguous place" (C. I. Lewis).[2]

Currently this discipline is virtually dead. British philosophy has foregone metaphysics generally, Continental philosophy the objectivity which traditionally has been so much a part of metaphysics that the definitions don't even trouble to mention it. America's contribution to the demise has been her metaphysically suspicious pragmatism. Before mid-century, R. G. Collingwood could describe our times as "an age . . . when the very possibility of metaphysics is hardly admitted without a struggle."[3] More recently Iris Murdoch has written: "Modern philosophy is profoundly anti-metaphysical in spirit. Its anti-metaphysical character may be summed up in the caveat: There may be no deep structure. This is the lesson of Wittgenstein."[4]

The roots of this suspicion run back— to Kierkegaard, Nietzsche, and Pascal on the Continent, and across the Channel to Hume. But these were men before their time. It has remained for our generation to see as a generation the import of their prophecies. A-cosmism at large, lapping at the shores of thought's entire empire, streaming into the inlets of every specialized discipline, breaking into spray which salts the eyes of even the man on the boardwalk—a-cosmism in these proportions is a twentieth-century discovery.

In England the wave crested in logical positivism's "elimination of metaphysics" proclamation and has rolled on thereafter in the analytic movement. Of the two, positivitism said the ruder things about metaphysics, but only because it defined "metaphysics" and "meaning" in ways that made them disjunctive. Actually it was less skeptical than its successors have been, for it assumed that the world does have a structure and that philosophy can perfect a language which, as used to order the findings of science, can picture it without distortion. The "ordinary language" movement doubts both points, assuming that it is profitable neither to ask after the structure of reality in general nor to dream of constructing a language governed by a single set of rules which is capable of doing justice to the full gamut of human experience and functionings.

Twentieth-century American philosophy has been equally a-cosmic. Reviewing Dewey's *Experience and Nature* Santayana asked, ". . . how comes it that . . . cosmology is absent from his system, and that every natural fact becomes in his hands so strangely unseizeable and perplexing?" His answer is: Because of "the dominance of the foreground . . . Nature is here not a world but a story."[5] Or rather, many stories? Speaking to "The Way the World Is," Nelson Goodman concludes that "the world is many ways. . . . There is no way which is the way the world is. . . . But there are many ways the world is, and every true description captures one of them."[6]

The existentialists on the Continent agree with this. Stressing to the extent they do that man is his relation to his situation, they are emphatic in insisting that as the life situations men occupy differ markedly, traditional metaphysics' dream of a single world outlook relevant to everyone is misguided in principle. But they go on from here to make another point. Whereas British philosophy has tended to see metaphysics as rationally deficient—where not actually meaningless, then at least fatty or sloppy—Continental philosophy sees it as too rational, too intellectual. For being cannot be laid before the mind as if it were an object. To the extent that it can be known at all, our knowledge of it must be of a special sort in which experience, with which thought must always be meshed to some degree, deepens to the point where the dichotomy between subject and object is transcended.

II

How are we to account for this near stampede from the endeavor which historically has been philosophy's central concern? The social turmoil of our century may have played some part; also the extraordinary increase in our knowledge of history and cultural anthropology by making us aware of how variously the world can be, and under various skies has been, conceived. But these have been contributing causes at most. The central cause has been honesty.

Neither of the two directions in which metaphysicians have proceeded in their attempt to build their world views looks promising today. The deductive method used indubitable starting points—irreducible units of experience or self-evident principles of reason—as launching pads from which logic was projected to outline what was supposed to be being's necessary structure. The inductive method surveyed the full arc of man's experience and attempted to abstract therefrom characteristics (categories) which unite, divide, and structure.

How can we retain our faith in either approach today? Deductive metaphysics founders on the fact that there are no indubitable starting points; cogitos, matter/form dichotomies, sense data, all have been found to be open to intelligent questionings. This discovery unmasks deductive metaphysics' conclusions of their presumed certainty and throws them into camp with those of the economic analyst who takes a rough hunch and refines it to the seventh decimal place. Meanwhile the findings of inductive metaphysics command equally little conviction. The difficulty here arises not only from the deluge of information which, as a consequence of the systematization and subsidy of research has poured in upon us faster than we have been able to order it.[a] The problem is oc-

---

[a] Approximately two million scientific experiments are now being reported each year, and it has been estimated that the quantity of factual information in virtually every academic discipline is doubling about every ten years.

casioned as much by the puzzling character of the new facts as by their number: particles that behave counter-intuitively; ostensibly objective experiments that are affected by the experimenter's expectations;[b] thoughts that appear to transmit themselves without physical media,[c] and so on. In the absence of convincing syntheses to order the facts within departments of knowledge individually, how can we hope for a purview that will order them all? If Toynbee failed, what hope for a metaphysician?

These thoughts weigh heavily; so heavily that we might be tempted to abandon metaphysics forever, or at least for the time being, were it not for one fact. This fact is the nature of man. Man's knowing seems to reach out for something in the direction of metaphysics, and his life, which includes more than knowing, seems to as well.

III

Begin with life. Anthropologists have found that human life in the aggregate, which is to say human cultures, invariably include embracing outlooks on life and the world which provide their members with a sense of where they are and what is required of them. Psychologists find equal evidence of needs in this direction as they consider persons individually rather than in groups. Erich Fromm says all persons need "a frame of orientation." William Sheldon makes the point more emphatically. "Continued observations . . . in clinical psychological practice," he writes, "lead almost inevitably to the conclusion that deeper and more fundamental than sexuality, deeper than the craving for social power, deeper even than the desire for possessions, there is a still more generalized and more universal craving in the human makeup. It is the craving for knowledge of the right direction—for orientation."

I find mid-century British and (to a large extent) American philosophers puzzling in their stance toward this need. They acknowledge that "man is a creature who makes pictures of himself and then comes to resemble the picture,"[7] while conveying the impression

---

[b] The allusion is to Dr. Rosenthal's experiment at the University of North Dakota in which he assigned undifferentiated rats to his assistants telling some that they were being given genius rats and others that they were being given stupid ones with the result that the "genius" rats learned to run mazes markedly faster than did the "stupid" ones.

[c] Cf. C. D. Broad's attempt, which he admits comes to naught, to render an intelligible explanation for telepathy. *Religion, Philosophy, and Psychical Research* (New York: Harcourt, Brace & Co., 1953), chap. 2.

that philosophy's historic involvement in such picture painting, alongside that of theology and art, is no longer becoming. One of our most judicious philosophers recently extolled a deceased colleague as a man "not . . . driven by a theological concern for the place of man in the scheme of things. Philosophy as he practiced it does not yield solace to bruised spirits; and it offers no apocalyptic vision of the universe, or a unified system of principles that provide categorical answers." The implication is that attempts to locate man in his cosmic setting are compensations for intellectual or emotional weakness.

If any one of the following propositions is true, the current Anglo-American unconcern with overviews is justified:

1. The need for overviews is apparent only, not real.

2. The need for overviews may in some instances be genuine, but where it is thus genuine it is pathological. Consequently attention should be directed to removing the need rather than catering to it. (John Wisdom?)

3. Overviews may be important, but reason can indicate nothing regarding them. They arise from faith, circumstance, chance, or naked decision. (Kierkegaard?)

4. Overviews may be important and reason competent in principle to work with them, but not yet. The premise here is that knowledge proceeds from part to whole; until we have clarified our understanding of aspects of experience that impinge on us directly and elementally, how can we hope to deal significantly with imponderables? (G. E. Moore?[8] Also Gilbert Ryle?[9])

But none of these propositions is true. The fourth is the most plausible, but the tide has turned against even it. Whether we listen to psychology, phenomenology, or the philosophy of science, the report is the same: there is no datum unpatterned, no figure without ground, no fact without theory. Psychology abandoned atomism with its discovery that there is no level of experience, perceptual or otherwise, that is free from what positivism called noncognitive factors, and other epistemologically interested disciplines have followed suit with varying degrees of alacrity. Instead of a one-way process whereby through perceptual archaeology irrefrangible primitive elements—Hume's impressions, Russell's and Moore's sense data—are first spotted and then built into wholes, knowledge (we now see) is polar. Part and whole are in dialogue from the start.

And because this is so, philosophers cannot ignore metaphysics even if they abandon existential questions to psychologists and theologians forthwith. As long as they retain their interest in epistemology, questions of unrestricted scope (i.e., metaphysical questions) will inevitably intrude. For no man looks at the world with pristine eyes; he sees it edited, and editorial policy is always forged in the widest field of vision at command.

IV

If this is true, we should expect to find philosophers' recent attempts to take their epistemology "neat" proving unsuccessful. And this, in fact, we do find. It is now generally agreed that the positivists were metaphysical with a vengeance.[10] As for their linguistic successors, if we take Gilbert Ryle as a sample can we not paraphrase Lenin's charge that "in Huxley agnosticism serves as a fig-leaf for materialism" and say that in Ryle ordinary language philosophy serves as a cover for behaviorism? Phenomenology's careful methodology has been no more successful in screening the biases of its practitioners. Husserl thought that "bracketing" existence would enable us to read off given phenomena in a presuppositionless way, but are we to believe that no assumptions intervened between his bracketing and his conclusion that consciousness constitutes the world? Heidegger and Sartre posit a direct, unreflective knowing through mood and affect. But do the moods of somberness, hopelessness, and bitter, ascetic heroism through which they predominantly view the human predicament (why not, as Paul Pruyser has asked, simply the human situation?) do nothing to color (discolor?) the reality pictures that emerge from them? Are we to take it as accidental that the contemporary phenomenologist who does most justice to the joyous side of man's existence and his hope, namely, Marcel, is the one who approaches his subject from an expressly Christian orientation? Apparently the attempt to elucidate being-in-general from being-human contains no inbuilt protection against the danger of generalizing from the way being-human strikes a particular phenomenologist. De Waelhens saw this twenty years ago when he wrote that "so-called neutral descriptions are full of moral and philosophical presuppositions—phenomenology is often a 'point of view' rather than pure description."[11]

V

I suspect that as our century draws toward its close metaphysical interest will quicken to such an extent that rebirth will appear a not inapposite metaphor. I say this not only because I agree with Kant in his *Critique of Pure Reason* that men have a psychological need to ask the overarching questions but also for logical reasons as well. It is one of the ironies of our time—completely understandable, but ironical nonetheless—that rising standards of scholarship and the explosion of knowledge have fragmented research in every field at precisely the moment that we see most clearly that knowing always involves a convergence between elements and the contexts that endow them with meaning. We are doing well with the elements. In the decades ahead philosophical endeavor will reflect a growing realization of the limited usefulness of advancing on this front while marking time on the other.[12]

What pointers might guide us as our interest in metaphysics revives?

1. No longer should we expect our systems to mirror the noumenal world (a) in its fullness or (b) even in limited features it may possess in itself. We have come to know too much about the relativity of knowledge to continue the traditional metaphysical ambition of bringing our thoughts into isomorphic congruence with reality as it exists apart from our perspectives. Insofar as we now think of reality-as-it-is-in-itself at all, we are inclined to imagine it as an un-ordered phenomenal wilderness—along the lines of Merleau-Ponty's "pre-objective world," perhaps, or the "buzzing, booming confusion" of the infantile mind as James envisioned it. Against this amorphous background we build our "coherent fairy tales." From now on we shall regard any view of reality we construct as being the way it appears from the human perspective.

2. Or rather, "from *a* human perspective," we are likely to add in view of our greater awareness of the variety of ways in which the world can take shape in men's minds in different times and places. But it is important here to distinguish three levels at which world views can be attempted. (a) There may be some generic features which all world views must possess by virtue of the fact that they are framed by human beings. Crosscultural studies, from perception and linguistics right over into comparative mythology, would ap-

pear to be the best means of discerning these features insofar as they exist. (b) Other elements in our outlooks will not be required by our basic humanity but instead will derive their plausibility from a given cultural heritage: what it "knows" about the world, its criteria of credibility, its prevailing assumptions, and dominant expectations. (c) Finally, there are features of our outlooks which are, and should remain, idiosyncratic. A phrase, a metaphor, a mantram, each for reasons that are entirely personal might organize the world meaningfully for some individual without the slightest claim to do so for others.

Generic, cultural, and personal aspects of world views—traditional metaphysics has focused on the first, existentialism on the other two. There is place for all three.

3. Wittgenstein's release of meaning from reference into use opens important possibilities for help from those who approach philosophy through linguistic analysis. I have yet to see an adequate statement of the valid uses of metaphysical discourse; even theological discourse seems to have received greater attention. A careful analysis of the functions and rules of metaphysical assertions should prove most valuable.

4. Along the lines just mentioned, analytic philosophy can help. It has another side, however, which is less auspicious. This is the side that gets tangled with the notion that philosophy is concerned exclusively with questions of form rather than content. The first (positivistic) version of this notion was grounded in the distinction between analytic and synthetic: philosophy was to occupy itself exclusively with analytic issues while leaving synthetic ones to science. The second (Wittgensteinian) version draws the line between analyzing language games and using them for purposes other than such analysis; from there it goes on to suggest that the concerns of philosophy are exclusively with linguistic analysis. It is doubtful that either of these distinctions is airtight; and even if they were, they would truncate philosophy if used to restrict its scope. Metaphysics' task is not over when the nature of metaphysical discourse is specified or even when the major modes of discourse are disentangled. The problems of metaphysics are not coterminal with those of language unless language is equated with thought.

5. The error of supposing that we cannot profitably proceed to metaphysical questions until we get a number of smaller questions

answered has already been remarked. It involves the fallacy of thinking that knowledge proceeds uni-directionally from part to whole. Kenneth Boulding's *The Image*[13] does a nice job of showing the extent to which throughout the various domains of knowledge our identification, valuation, and interpretation of data is controlled by our images of wholes. The attics of university buildings are crammed with research files which lie abandoned for eternity because changes in hypotheses render their data irrelevant. Meaning descends from whole to part as much as it ascends from part to whole.

6. The existentialist and phenomenological suspicions of objectivity and system need to be pondered carefully. They fear the right things—cynicism, relativism, nihilism—but have they correctly diagnosed their causes? "You cannot get everything into your system unless you have first gotten everything out of your system," they say, punning on the word "system" to make the point that to conceptualize a problem is to divorce oneself from it emotionally. But is this true—of Spinoza, of Saint Thomas, of some Marxists and Vedantists I know today? Eric Heller says that the health of a culture (and by implication an individual) is determined by the number of values it takes so much for granted that it isn't even aware of them. This criterion makes every Hottentot healthier than Socrates. If existentialists and phenomenologists discover a method of building engagement into the very fabric of their theses, this will be a remarkable breakthrough: one which neither poets nor religious writers have thus far managed. Short of this, we will do better to strive for good systems and the kind of objectivity that is not incompatible with commitment than to abjure these attributes of metaphysics while having no alternatives.

VI

As to the mode by which a new metaphysics might emerge, one thinks of two possibilities. If a dramatic new truth about the world were to come into view; if, in the succession of the Copernican revolution, Darwinian evolution, Freudianism, or quantum mechanics, we were tomorrow to become completely convinced that extrasensory perception, say, is a reality, or if we were to discover life on other planets so radically different that it threw the question of what life is into an entirely new perspective—if revolutionary discoveries of proportions such as these were to come into view I suspect that interest would swing rapidly from many of our present minute concerns toward working out the implications of the new discoveries for our view of life and reality in general. Short of this, the best prospect would seem to be to keep a careful eye on the basic concepts and theories of the various major fields of knowledge and try to formulate a general scheme of categories which will provide a perspective in which to view them all.

My single confidence is that the conviction to which Professor Hartshorne has devoted his intellectual life—that metaphysics is philosophy's central concern—will before long again be widespread in the philosophical community.

NOTES

1. *Process and Reality* (New York: Macmillan Company, 1941), p. 4.
2. *Mind and the World Order* (New York: Charles Scribner's Sons, 1929), p. 12.
3. *An Essay on Metaphysics* (Oxford: Oxford University Press, 1940), p. 224.
4. In D. F. Pears, ed., *The Nature of Metaphysics* (London: Macmillan and Co., 1956), p. 109.
5. Bernard Suits, "Naturalism: Half-Hearted or Broken-Backed?" *Journal of Philosophy* 68, no. 7 (30 March 1961): 169.
6. *Review of Metaphysics* 14, no. 1 (September 1960): 55.
7. Iris Murdoch, in D. F. Pears, *The Nature of Metaphysics*, p. 122.
8. Professor Nagel has reminded us that Moore "never associated himself . . . with current revolts against the traditional conception of philosophy as an inquiry into the most general features of the entire scheme of things" ("The Debt We Owe to G. E. Moore," *Journal of Philosophy*, 67 [22 December 1960]: 811). On the contrary, he maintained that one of the tasks of philosophy is to present "a general description of the whole of the universe" (G. E. Moore, *Some Main Problems of Philosophy* [London: Allen & Unwin, 1953], p. 1). But he was convinced that such descriptions can command respect only when compiled or extrapolated from accurate knowledge of the world's parts. "That all truths about the universe possess to one another all the various relations which may be meant by 'unity', can only be legitimately asserted, when we have carefully distinguished those various relations and discovered what those truths are" (*Principia Ethica* [Cambridge: Cambridge University Press, 1954], p. 222).
9. Our critics "scold us . . . for our sedulous refusal to talk about the cosmos. . . . To this charge we had better plead guilty, though not, I suggest, with grave dejection. The time is not yet ripe for new global syntheses" (in D. F. Pears, *The Nature of Metaphysics*, p. 156).
10. Professor Hartshorne was among the first to point this out. See his "Metaphysics for Positivists," *Philosophy of Science* 2, no. 3 (July 1935): 287–303.

11. *La philosophie de Martin Heidegger* (Louvain: Edit. de l'institut Supérieur de Philosophie, 1942).

12. Already there are harbingers of recovery. Findlay's *Hegel*, Strawson's *Individuals*, and Hampshire's *Thought and Action* all go beyond piecemeal studies in the direction of syntheses, and it is said that toward the close of his life even Austin was coming around to more general questions in his Saturday morning discussions.

13. Ann Arbor: University of Michigan Press, 1956.

Part Two

A CLEARING

Fifteen years separate the preceding essays from the ones that follow (save for the last one, which is a kind of coda), and the two sets differ markedly in character. Whereas the earlier essays were written out of concern over the absence of an integrating outlook, an absence that has produced (in Peter Berger's telling title) *The Homeless Mind,* the later ones critique the inadequacies of a part of the Post-Modern Mind—roughly speaking the mind of the university—that is integrated but in a way that constricts.

What brought the latter to light was the crystallizing of a point of view of my own. When my own thoughts acquired form, the way they contrasted—sharply, consistently, and eventually predicably—with those around me showed that the latter had form too. I describe my point of view in *Forgotten Truth: The Primordial Tradition,* which was written during the interval mentioned; the statement that constitutes this second part of the book in hand reviews its key points, mostly in new ways, and presents a running commentary on them. Written expressly for this present book, it is designed to throw a bridge from the largely descriptive essays of part one to the more critical and prescriptive ones that follow it.

"There is no reply, in clear terrain, to an archer under cover," the medievalist Dorothy Dunnet has written. As the remaining essays rain arrows on the Modern Western Mind-set, it is only fair to indicate where they come from. Equally important, the disclosure of my own premises should make the critiques that flow from them more intelligible.

·3·

PERENNIAL PHILOSOPHY,
PRIMORDIAL TRADITION

An indication of how the outlook to be described broke over me may help to highlight some of its features, so I shall use this way of moving into it.

Early resonance to the writings of Gerald Heard had led me to his friend Aldous Huxley and the mosaic of mysticism the latter had put together under the title *The Perennial Philosophy*. In his introduction to that book Huxley notes that though it was Leibniz who coined the phrase *philosophia perennis,* the thing itself—"the metaphysic that recognizes a divine Reality substantial to the world of things and lives and minds; the psychology that finds in the soul something similar to, or even identical with, divine Reality; the ethic that places man's final end in the knowledge of the immanent and transcendent Ground of all being—is immemorial and universal. Rudiments of the Perennial Philosophy," he continues,

> may be found among the traditionary lore of primitive peoples in every region of the world, and in its fully developed forms it has a place in every one of the higher religions. A version of this Highest Common Factor in all preceding and subsequent theologies was first committed to writing more than twenty-five centuries ago, and since that time the inexhaustible theme has been treated again and again, from the standpoint of every religious tradition and in all the principal languages of Asia and Europe.[1]

For twenty-five years I had known of this position and even sensed theoretically that it lay in the right direction, but it took a

sequence of concrete events to bring me face to face with it, whereupon it quickly took over. I had known that certain contemporary
thinkers such as Ananda Coomaraswamy and René Guénon stood
in direct line with the writers Huxley had anthologized, but it was
Frithjof Schuon's books that caused the familiar to jump to my
attention as if I were seeing it with new eyes. I tell the story in my
introduction to the revised edition of Schuon's *Transcendent Unity
of Religions,* but retell it here for purposes at hand.

It was the autumn of 1969, and I was embarking on an academic
year around the world. Of the decisions as to what to include in my
forty-four-pound luggage limit, the final one concerned a book that
had just crossed my desk: *In the Tracks of Buddhism* by Frithjof
Schuon. I barely recognized his name, but the book's middle section,
entitled "Buddhism's Ally in Japan: Shinto or the Way of the
Gods," caught my eye. Two weeks later, at our first stop, Japan, I
would have to be lecturing on Shinto and I had little feel for its
outlook. I badly needed an entrée, so I wedged the book into my
bulging flight bag.

It proved to be the best decision of the year. Before the sacred
shrine at Ise, symbolic center of the nation of Japan, under its giant
cryptomeria and at low tables in its resthouse for pilgrims, the Way
of the Gods opened before me. Ise's atmosphere itself could be cred-
ited with the unveiling, but only if I add that it was Schuon's insights
that enabled me to sense within that atmosphere—it's dignity, beauty, and repose—an intellective depth. I came to see how ancestors
could appear less fallen than their descendants and thereby serve,
when revered, as doorways to transcendence. I saw how virgin
nature—especially in its grand phenomena: sun, wind, moon, thunder, lightning, and the sky and earth that are their containers—
could be venerated as the most transparent symbols of the divine.
Above all, I saw how Shinto, indigenous host for "the Japanese
miracle," could be seen as the most intact instance of an archaic
hyperborean shamanism that swept from Siberia across the Bearing Straits to the Native Americans.

Two months later, in India, the same thing happened. Perusing a
bookstore in Madras, my eye fell on a study of the Vedanta entitled
Language of the Self, again by Frithjof Schuon. This time I didn't
hesitate. The remaining weeks in India were spent with that book
under my arm, and I was happy. A decade's tutelage under a swami

of the Ramakrishna Order had familiarized me with the basic Vedantic outlook, but Schuon took off from there as if from base camp, while showing at each step, through a stunning series of cross-references, how the Vedantic profundities were Indic variations on themes that are universal because grounded in man's inherent nature as related to his Source.

Would one believe a third installment? In Iran the leading Islamicist pointed me to Schuon's *Understanding Islam* as "the best work in English on the meaning of Islam and why Muslims believe in it." I had been to East Asia, South Asia, and West Asia, and in each the same personage had surfaced to guide and illumine. The point, though, is not the person or the particular books that crossed my path but rather the position they articulated.

The feature of that position that grasped me was the way it joined universality to final truth. Of these two, truth is the more important, but its insistence that no human collectivity has been without it (an insistence so strong that the words "primordial" and "perennial" are built into its very name) made me listen intently to what was being said, for I was caught up in the issue. As missionaries to China, my parents and grandparents had given their lives to taking truth to those who lacked it, whereas my crosscultural eyes had accommodated better to truths other peoples already possess.[a] How much my upbringing in another culture set the stage I do not know, but what was clear was that, though I had delighted in cultural differences, I had not been able to absolutize them. Training under swamis, Zen masters, and Sufi shaikhs; encountering Tiwis and Aruntas in the Australian bush; sitting in total harmony with Thomas Merton, the Dalai Lama, and a remarkable Native American chief on the nearby Onondaga reservation, I had felt the same still presence.

---

[a] This sentence is not intended to disown the missionary enterprise. Last March I attended a service of worship in a church my family frequented in the 1920s and 30s when we passed through Shanghai. Two thousand parishioners were in attendance. In addition to the sanctuary which was packed, sixteen amplified Sunday school rooms were overflowing and the minister pled with the congregation not to attend church more than once on a Sunday because doing so deprived others of the privilege. To gaze on the faces in that congregation, many streaming with tears, while remembering the twenty-eight years of persecution the church in China had suffered before its doors had been permitted to reopen two years before my visit, was to know that Christianity was providing at least these people with something their indigenous tradition did not, and perhaps to them could not. This is to say nothing of the incalculable debt I myself owe to dedicated Indian, Japanese, Tibetan, and Islamic teachers who have made America their mission field.

What I did not know was how to give it words, and the perennial philosophy showed me how. Because the words were in "esperanto," so to speak, their claimed universality merits another two paragraphs.

I think we can now see that the radical existentialist claim that man has no nature ("existence precedes essence") was an exaggeration to make a point; the givens in human existence cannot be discounted this easily. By definition we all partake of these givens—we are all more human than otherwise, someone has remarked—and as intelligence is one of them, it stands to reason that in pondering our commonalities, thoughtful persons everywhere would have gravitated toward similar conclusions. If we approach the point by way of revelation instead of human discovery, the result is the same. That God, while desiring the well-being of his children, should have left the vast majority of them (including the most gifted) to stagnate for thousands of years, practically without hope, in the darkness of mortal ignorance until he chose to disclose his truth to a rivulet of humanity concentrated in a tiny locale, this "scandal of particularity" (if I have rightly stated its essence) is too monstrous to abide. "To suppose that God could act in such a manner . . . flagrantly contradicts [his] nature, the essence of which is Goodness and Mercy. This nature, as theology is far from being unaware, can be 'terrible' but not monstrous."[2] Saint Augustine's doctrine of "Wisdom uncreate, the same now as it ever was and ever will be," is more generous and becoming, as is his conclusion that this Wisdom came to be called Christianity only after the coming of Christ. According to an esoteric exegesis of Genesis 11:1, the primordial or unanimous tradition goes back to the single spiritual language which, with the Tower of Babel, splintered into multiple but parallel dialects.

The obvious problem the claim of unanimity must face is the differences that traditions also display. Some thinkers are so occupied with these differences that they dismiss claims of commonality as simply sloppy thinking, yet identity *within* difference is as common an experience as life affords. Green is not blue, yet both are light. A gold watch is not a gold ring, but both are gold. Women are not men, but both are human. Everything turns on which foot one comes down on. And as that cannot be decided by logic, we need to bring in content to determine which "foot" deserves to be emphasized. That the truth in question has been ubiquitous—"the living God . . . in . . . all nations . . . left not himself without witness" (Acts 14:15–17)—is in its favor, but it is not that which makes it either important or true.

I have already quoted Aldous Huxley's characterization of the perennial philosophy as

> the metaphysic that recognizes a divine Reality substantial to the world of things and lives and minds; the psychology that finds in the soul something similar to, or even identical with, divine Reality; the ethic that places man's final end in the knowledge of the immanent and transcendent Ground of all being,

and as I cannot imagine a better brief summation, I shall let my own exposition take the form of a commentary on these three basic themes.

1. METAPHYSICS

The Metaphysic that recognizes a divine Reality substantial to the world of things and lives and minds.

The perennial philosophy is emphatically ontological, which is to say that its overriding concern is with being (*on* in Greek). Heidegger says that the West has forgotten the question of being, and on the whole he is right. The collapse of metaphysics which the opening essay in this book describes is the clearest sign of this forgetting, along with the concomitant rise to preeminence of topics which, though important, should rightfully remain ancillary: epistemology, language, and questions of method. "A loss or weakening of the metaphysical spirit is an incalculable damage for the general order of intelligence and human affairs," Jacques Maritain wrote around mid-century,[3] and so it is. As our fate is totally dependent on the matrix that produced and sustains us, interest in its nature is the holiest interest that can visit us.

A key feature of that nature, according to the perennial philosophy, is its hierarchical character.[b] In outlining his own notion of the

---

[b] "The ability to see the Great Truth of the hierarchic structure of the world, which makes it possible to distinguish between higher and lower Levels of Being, is one of the indispensable conditions of understanding" (E. F. Schumacher, *A Guide for the Perplexed*, p. 14).

universe as a "holarchy," a hierarchy of holons or self-maintaining entities that are parts of larger wholes, Arthur Koestler admits that "hierarchy is an ugly word. Loaded with ecclesiastical and military associations, [it] conveys to some people a wrong impression of a rigid or authoritarian structure." But misunderstandings and possible abuses, he goes on to say, should not blind us to the fact that "all complex structures and processes of relatively stable character display hierarchic organization, and this applies regardless whether we are considering inanimate systems, living organisms, social organizations, or patterns of behavior."[4] "The almost universal applicability of the hierarchic model" that Koestler points to (p. 291) is obvious in the empirical world, but the metaphysical point is that it is not likely that it would figure so prominently there if it were not embedded in the structure of reality itself.

> The conception of the universe as . . . ranging in hierarchical order from the meagerest kind of existents . . . through "every possible" grade up to the *ens perfectissimum* . . . has, in one form or another, been the dominant official philosophy of the larger part of civilized mankind through most of its history.[c]

The different grades that are mentioned in this quotation are analogous to the levels of size in inanimate matter (as encountered in quantum mechanics, chemistry, daily life, and astronomy) and the degrees of complexity in organic life (plant, animal, and human). In each domain or kingdom we find distinctive properties and laws that hold for its population but not others; they define the region in question and distinguish it from its neighbors. In philosophy categories are used to sort out classes of things that need to be distinguished, and the phrase "category mistake" has caught on to signal the confusion that results when their differences are neglected. The distinctive claim of the perennial philosophy, as the quotation from Lovejoy brings out, is that the categories of existents—the classes of kinds of things that exist—are hierarchically ordered. Reality is tiered; being increases as the levels ascend. Ascent is used here figuratively, of course. No literal up, or spatial move whatever, is involved.

---

[c] Arthur Lovejoy, *The Great Chain of Being* (Cambridge: Harvard University Press, 1936), pp. 59, 26.

We must attend carefully here, for this is the step in the argument which, though it was commonplace to the point of being universal in the past, is the most difficult for modern consciousness to grasp. What can it mean to say that X has more being than Y; or in ordinary parlance, that it is more real?

Plato's allegory of the cave is the classic effort to tell us. The shadows its chained prisoners see are certainly real in that they exist in some sense and to some degree, but the objects that cast them are more substantial and, in this sense, embody more existence. In possessing three dimensions rather than two, in outlasting their shadows and manifesting more independence generally, three-dimensional objects possess in greater abundance properties that things must possess to some extent if they are to exist at all. When one of the prisoners manages to escape from Plato's cave, the privative character of shadows becomes even more evident for shadows are nothing but the relative absence *of* light—the light that can then be directly seen.

To ring a change on Plato's allegory: I enter a room and see my wife. No, it turns out not to be her; it is her reflection in a wall-size mirror. The reflection exists, but it is certainly not my wife. And it is manifestly less than my wife. If it be objected that it is less real as wife but not as reflection, the answer is that it is the former that is at issue. That her reflection falls short of her full selfhood is (we are asked to think) analogous to the ways some beings fall short of others. The difficult part, of course, is to imagine things that are more real than the three-dimensional objects that stand before us in clear daylight. Perhaps it will help if, staying with the example of my wife, we try to imagine a perception that could encompass her entire history—each moment exactly as she lived it but collapsed in a way that enabled me to take them all in an instant. If in some magical way the dimension of time were thus added to the three that are now evident, the wife I now see would by comparison seem abstract in the way her two-dimensional reflection is abstract now. To my newly endowed eyes her three-dimensional self would be only the surface of her complete, longitudinal self that the added time dimension placed before me like a four-dimensional "block."

The point of fanciful moves like these is to try to breathe life into the possibility that we are not the highest octave in being's register. There are things that exceed us, and the things our senses report, in the way objects exceed shadows and wives their mirror images. Obviously we are surrounded by objects that exceed us *in certain respects*—mountains outlast us in duration and lightning packs more power—but the claim of the great chain of being, which can be taken as the perennial philosophy's ontological spine (or better, spire), is that positive attributes go together: increase one and the others burgeon concomitantly. That the longevity of mountains does not make them wise any more than lightning's power makes it long-lasting is no refutation of that claim, for it concerns deep structures only. Lightning and mountains belong to the same level of reality, the physical, and on any single level qualities group and regroup in all manner of ways to allow for variety. It is only in crossing ontic lines, in ways analogous to passing from the quantum to the atomic level in physics, that qualities keep step with one another. And we can see why this lockstep is important. To Ernst Haeckel's question of questions, "Is the universe friendly?", religion answers, finally yes; in William James's formulation, "religion says that the best things are the more eternal things, the things in the universe that throw the last stone, so to speak, and say the final word."[5] Three categories are aligned in this statement, all in their exemplary modes: value (the best things), time (the more eternal things), and power (the things that throw the last stone). In a completely meaningful world they *must* thus converge, for the only fully satisfactory explanation for the way things are is that they should be that way. The charge that attention to teleological considerations of this sort reduces the perennial philosophy to a rationale for wishful thinking will be dealt with in the "Flakes of Fire" essay in part three, but we can anticipate what will be said there to the extent of a single sentence. As the hypothesis that this is a good world and that fuller understanding will carry us beyond appearances to the contrary is the most fruitful working hypothesis there is, comparable in metaphysics to science's working premise that cancer has a cause even if it is not yet known, to explore this hypothesis energetically is a sign of health rather than pathology as long as facts are not blinked *en route*.

Thus far the claim of a tiered reality has been broached through images, but it can be stated literally if we are willing to accept abstractions. To have more being, or be more real, is to possess more of the properties of being per se. These include:

a. Power. It may be miniscule, but it is present. Plato seems to have been the first to have said that to exist is to exert influence. If there were something to which nothing responded, it would not register at all and we would have no reason to assume it exists. "What is it to be 'real'?" William James asked, and answered, "The best definition I know is: 'Anything is real of which we find ourselves obliged to take into account in any way.'"[6] It has the power to make its presence felt.

b. Duration.

c. Locale.

d. Unity. What exists can have parts and usually does, but unless these cohere in a way that gives it an identifiable integrity, *it* cannot be said to exist; only the components do.

e. Importance. Again this may be small, but to exist to any degree is to count for something.

f. Worth. If nothing is better than something, there is no basis for discussion. *Esse qua esse bonum est;* being as being is good.

Other properties may be required, but these suffice for our purpose. We have been asking what it would mean for X to possess them in higher degree than Y, but to sharpen the contrast we can change "higher" to "highest." If X's power were infinite, it would be *omnipotent*. If its duration had no cutoff, it would be *eternal*. If its locale were without bounds, it would be *omnipresent*. If its unity were uncompromised, it would be *simple* in the technical sense of harboring no divisions whatever. If its importance were utter, it would be *absolute*. If its worth were categorical, it would be *perfect*.

These are, of course, the attributes of God, and all theists will subscribe to a hierarchy of two levels (God and the world), as will metaphysicians who distinguish in some way between the absolute and the relative. A simple dichotomy, though, is inadequate for the distinctions that are needed; both God and the world must be qualified, God by separating his knowable from his unknowable aspects, the world by distinguishing its invisible from its visible features. For to repeat the criteria that require levels to be demarcated in the first place, each of the four we now have in view—God manifest, God unmanifest; world visible, world invisible—has an importantly distinct population and distinctive ways in which its members interact. The number four oversimplifies—the number may actually be indefinite—but these four broad divisions, appearing as they do explicity in all known civilizations and implicitly in virtually every studied tribe, appear to be the minimum that collectivities must respect if their outlooks are to mesh reasonably with the way things are. Individuals can get along with less than four, but not societies if they are to accommodate the full range of spiritual personality types that surface everywhere. My *Forgotten Truth* takes the description of the four levels as its primary task; here they can only be identified. A supplementing identification appears in the essay "Excluded Knowledge" on pages 73–75. The reader may wish to glance ahead to it, for both descriptions are brief and together they may deepen the view like a stereopticon.

Listed in the order of diminishing reality as the eye moves down the page, the four principal levels of existence are the following:

God unmanifest: Godhead or the Infinite.

God manifest: the celestial plane.

The world in its invisible aspects: mind and the vital principle;
the intermediate plane.[d]

The world as (in principle) visible: space, time, and matter; the
terrestrial plane.

As the God/world distinction is relatively standard, I shall ride on it and identify the four levels by the additional cuts that are needed on each side of that initial divide. In *Forgotten Truth* I distinguished God from the Godhead (Boehme's *ungrund;* Tillich's God-above-God: Eckhart uses the word Godhead itself) by defining the former as personal and the latter transpersonal, but this now strikes me as a tactical mistake. It is not wrong, but we have so much difficulty imagining anything superior to persons that, whatever is actually said, the impression that is conveyed in denying the attribute "per-

---

[d] Obviously the terms "visible" and "invisible" refer here not merely to the ocular sense but to all of our senses of outward observation. The powers of life, consciousness, and self-awareness are entirely invisible (without color, sound, taste, or smell) while being—this is important—what we are mainly interested in. All our thoughts, emotions, feelings, imaginations, reveries, dreams, fantasies, are invisible, and this has implications that are more startling than we normally realize. As it is these interior features that we identify with most—take ourselves at heart to be—we are invisible; we live in a world of invisible people. I have not chosen that way of putting the matter for its shock value. No verbal legerdemain is involved; only the insistence that we face the implications of the way we actually, workingly, think of ourselves. It would be an oversimplification to say that we are completely invisible, for we do have bodies; but as between oversimplifications, it is literally more accurate to say that we are invisible than to say the opposite.

sonal" to the Godhead is that it must be subpersonal, rather than
suprapersonal as the distinction intends. This misunderstanding can
be avoided if we draw the line instead between aspects of divinity
our minds can grasp—its personal aspect included—and ones that
outdistance comprehension categorically. When, two paragraphs
above, the pinnacle of being was said to be omnipresent, eternal,
and the like, God was in focus. In the Godhead these superlatives
are not withdrawn; they are, rather, advanced beyond the range of
our imaginings and fused into a unity reason cannot penetrate.
There is an age when a child may look at you earnestly and deliver a
long, pleased speech in which the inflections of spoken English are
perfectly reflected, yet not a single syllable can be recognized. There
is no way you can tell the child that she has done marvels with the
melody but, since language also makes sense, she has not gotten
very far with it. Something like this is involved in the God to
Godhead move; the language of theism gets God's melody right, but
the sense that is hidden in his final depths eludes it. In technical
terms, God is the object of cataphatic theology, the *via affirmativa,*
whereas Godhead is the object of apophatic theology, the *via
negativa.* The line is not hard and fast, but priests and prophets tend
to focus on God, mystics on the Godhead. And the latter tell us that
in those rare, supernatural moments when the Godhead is directly
disclosed to man, what man then sees is that he cannot understand
its nature at all. It is not that depths of its nature remain opaque
and ineffable; its simplicity precludes ladling things out this way. Its
entire *nature* reposes in depth unfathomable. So the incomprehensi-
bility of the Godhead becomes evident at the precise moment that
its nature is most clearly apprehended—there is no way to state the
point less paradoxically. In the light of mystical vision the
Godhead's hiddenness is not dispelled; it appears. Not that there are
two Gods, of course. It is just that his single nature does not stop
where our minds do.

As we turn from God to the world, its material countenance greets
us most emphatically, yet we need only close our eyes to find ourselves in a totally different medium: the world of direct, immediate,
inner awareness. Idealists have tried to reduce matter to mind and
materialists the opposite, but neither has carried the day. The difference between inner and outer, subjective and objective, the living
and the dead, cannot easily be argued away. I shall not try to say

here where the line should be drawn between the terms in these pairs; a small run on the point appears on pages 74–75 below. Those who wish to pursue it further can turn to chapters three and four in *Forgotten Truth*. It is enough to say that the great chain of being places mind ahead of matter not only in its worth but in its power and extent as well. Thus it runs counter to current suppositions. The essays that follow argue that these suppositions derive from modernity's having tailored its outlook excessively to science which sees how far things can be (a) explained in terms of ones that are simpler, and (b) controlled by altering these simpler components. The attention to "upward causation" that results from this approach has rubbed off onto the modern outlook as a whole, causing it to assume that influence per se flows predominantly from less to more. Yet even in science we sometimes catch glimpses of the opposite possibility.

Item. Together with time and mass/energy, size (space) is a property of matter; things on the upper three realms do not have to conform to it. Yet power stands in inverse ratio to size. The well-founded law that the shorter the wavelength the larger the energy that is compressed into it, produces the conclusion that "in a thimbleful of vacuum there is more . . . energy than would be released by all the atomic bomb fuel in the universe."[7] Stated in terms of particles instead of waves,

> the amount of energy associated with light corpuscles increases *as the size is reduced*. . . . The energy necessary to create a proton is contained in a light pulse only about 10^{-13} centimeter in diameter. And the energy of a million protons would be contained in a light pulse a million times smaller.[8]

As this principle has "no theoretical limit" (Young), speculation races toward the prospect that the energy of something that has no size at all—God?—might be infinite.

Item. Turning from physics to biology, we find the Gaia Hypothesis suggesting that causation descends from the animate to the inanimate in a way we had not suspected. Standard evolutionary theory depicts life as threading its way upward in an environment that is its opposite in being dead. The Gaia Hypothesis reverses this, suggesting that the remarkable life-supporting stability and coherence of the biosphere make it more plausible to think of it as some sort of enormous developing embryo. The earth is itself a form of life, "a complex entity involving the Earth's biosphere, atmosphere, oceans and soil; the totality constituting a feedback or cybernetic system which seeks an optimal physical and chemical environment for life on this planet. The physical and chemical condition of the surface of the Earth, of the atmosphere, and of the oceans has been and is actively made fit and comfortable by the presence of life itself."[9] Lewis Thomas notes that this hypothesis

> is beginning to stir up a few signs of storm, and if it catches on, as I think it will, we will soon find the biological community split into fuming factions, one side saying that the evolved biosphere displays evidence of design and purpose, the other decrying such heresy (ibid.).

The underlying question is whether the less or the more has the greater influence, and I have included these two items from science because major shifts in perspective are difficult and help from every quarter is useful. In essential (if barest) outline, the primordial metaphysics is now before us. Before proceeding to the psychology and ethics that follow from it, let me state five features which, once this metaphysics had come to focus for me, I found impressive.

1. There is the sheer quantity of material it "gestalts" into a meaningful pattern. Its hierarchical character deserves much of the credit for this achievement, for chains of command are a proven way of introducing order into large numbers. An army without staff and line would be a mere rabble, and something of the same can be said of world views. The computer scientist Herbert Simon has described, in a parable, the efficiency that hierarchies make possible. Because it applies in its own way to the hierarchy in the great chain of being, the parable is worth inserting. Two watchmakers, Hora and Tempus, both make watches composed of a thousand parts each. Hora assembles his watches piece by piece, so when he drops a watch he is working on it falls to pieces and he must begin from scratch. Tempus, for his part, assembles subassemblies of ten parts each, joins ten of these to make a larger subassembly of a hundred units, and then joins ten of these to make a complete watch. If he drops a part he is working on he will have to repeat at most ten

assembling operations and possibly none. If we assume a ratio of one mishap in a hundred operations, it will take Hora four thousand times longer to assemble a watch; if Tempus can do it in a day, it will take Hora eleven years. And if, for mechanical parts we substitute amino acids, protein molecules, organelles, and so on, the ratio between time scales becomes astronomical.

The levels of reality in the great chain of being form an analogue to the assemblies and subassemblies of Hora's watch. Each can be studied separately, after which only a manageable number of moves are required to bring them into an ordered whole. The marvels of the *terrestrial* plane are being unveiled at an astonishing rate by the physical sciences. The *intermediate* realm adds life and consciousness; biology helps with the former, and for light on the latter we can turn to the durable findings of phenomenology, depth psychology, and parapsychology, as well as aspects of shamanism and folk religion. The theologies of the great traditions describe God's knowable nature (the *celestial* plane) from a variety of cultural angles, and the literature of mysticism carries the mind as far as it can journey into God's absolute and *infinite* depths. Is anything of importance omitted in this ontic list? All world views must take account of everything in some way, but many do so by denying the existence of things their rivals consider important. Is it only because the perennial philosophy strikes me as true that it seems more generous in this regard? It validates so much that peoples have lived by. Many philosophies have no place for parapsychology, Jungian archetypes, or even phenomenology; many theologies no place for mysticism, other religions, or what falls under the rubric of folk religion. In the perennial philosophy these are all accorded a respectful place; science too, of course. It is as if the perennial philosophy were to say to the others: You are right in what you affirm. Only what you deny needs rethinking.

2. Not that it is all things to all people. If "a place for everything" shows its generous side, the sequel it appends, "and everything in its place," reveals its uncompromising, adamantine edge. That the lesser things (the lower rungs of being) really are inferior—to say nothing of not being the whole story—is, in its eyes, true and therefore not finally negotiable. Those who do not believe that higher realms exist will naturally not accept this. Such disagreements are unavoidable—worlds were not made for one another—but better

serious controversy than a flaccid tolerance that places agreement ahead of truth. The point is: the perennial philosophy is not relativistic, and this is a second thing that feels right about it. In calling his epochal discovery "relativity" Einstein all but named our age, which is riddled with relativities of unbelievable variety,[e] but what he actually unearthed was its opposite: invariance—that which is absolute and reliable *despite* the apparent confusions, illusions, and contradictions produced by the relative motions or actions of gravity. It would have been better if Einstein had called his discovery "the invariance theory," as he considered doing, for not only is invariance more fundamental than the relativities it explains, it signals better what truth is after. "Timeless truth" sounds almost like a contradiction in terms today, but we need to believe that the truth we seek is rooted in the unchanging depths of the universe. For were it not, would it be worth the cost of the search, to say nothing of the cost it exacts once the discovery is made? More on the latter point in the section on ethics that follows.

3. Absolutes can lock one into a limited perspective, and as all perspectives *are* limited, some thinkers now nominate iconoclasm— the smashing of ideologies and all conceptual schemes—for the ruling virtue. This sounds a little like trying to run a farm by careful weeding and no planting, but the danger that prompts it is real, and the third thing that appeals to me in the perennial philosophy is the way it handles the issue. The problem—our need to believe while remaining open to better beliefs and what lies beyond belief altogether[f]—must be resolved existentially, through living it, but the guidelines the perennial philosophy proposes seem right. In insisting that the final reality, the infinite, is radically ineffable, it relativizes all concepts, formulations, and systems vis-à-vis *it*—the finger pointing at the moon is not the moon itself; "all things pass save for the face of God" (the Koran). Meanwhile the confident

[e] See, below, the section titled "The Possibility of Certitude" in Chapter 8.
[f] What lies beyond belief altogether! "The starkness of . . . an incommensurable split between, on the one side, *language and the world included in language,* and, on the other side, *the unsayable and the world as unsayable* (sheer existence, immediacy of content, voiceless physiognomies, confronting the *I*)" was Wittgenstein's central vision and lifelong obsession (Henry Le Roy Finch, *Wittgenstein: The Later Philosophy* [Atlantic Highlands, N.J.: Humanities Press, 1977], p. 242).

orientation life needs if it is to be lived well is met by saying that *within* the ballpark of outlooks and theories—at the human level the game of life must in part be played in that park—this outlook carries the day and will yield tomorrow only to fresh expressions.

4. This last statement may confirm a suspicion that could have been germinating for some time; namely, that the unchanging character of this philosophy—its static quality, if you will, as embossed in its very name, "perennial"—gives it a somewhat stagnant air. Where is the sense of intellectual excitement, the prospect of new worlds to discover? The answer brings us to the fourth feature of the perennial philosophy that I find convincing. No more in this philosophy than in any other is there the prospect of a stopping point in this life. The questions are *where* one wants to go and *with what,* one's mind only, or one's total self. In the domain of mind a distinction must be drawn between cumulative and noncumulative truth; we find the first kind in history and science where information snowballs, and the second kind in metaphysics, religion, and art where it does not. In the latter triumverate a restless, insatiable appetite for novelty is like compulsive eating—fed by a disordered drive. What, twenty-five hundred years later, do we know about evil that Job did not know? That the question is rhetorical in no way means that adventure and discovery disappear. Their place in noncumulative knowledge is as lively as anywhere, but they face in a different, more important, direction: toward a deeper understanding of truths that are inexhaustible, and beyond this—here we move from mind to the total self—to the seasoning of one's being so understanding may phase into realization. The reservoir of noncumulative knowledge no more needs augmenting than, in the eyes of Robert Coles, Research Professor of Psychiatry at Harvard University, the data bank of psychiatry requires increase. Fully aware that to question the need for more research in that field is the gravest heresy one can risk, Coles proceeds to ask:

> What will psychiatry ever know that it does not know now about the damage done by thoughtless, cruel parents to vulnerable children? What further "frontiers" do we really have to conquer, when it comes to such subjects as despair, brutality, envy?

His answer:

> There is not much left for us to discover about man's fantasies, dreams, wishes, and doubts. The dynamics are all on the table, and in a way were there before Freud ever came along, as he acknowledged more than once. . . . We know all there is to know.[10]

When this statement is placed beside the following for the perennial philosophy, the similarity on the underlying point is striking.

> Few topics are so unrewarding as conventional laments about the "researches of the human mind" never being satisfied; in fact everything has been said already, though it is far from being the case that everyone has always understood it. There can therefore be no question of presenting "new truths"; what is needed in our time . . . is to provide some people with keys fashioned afresh—keys no better than the old ones but merely more elaborated—in an eternal script in the very substance of man's spirit.[11]

5. A fifth feature of the perennial philosophy I found compelling will complete this list: its ontic exuberance. Today it is mostly the sciences that are exuberant as they unveil a nature extravagant beyond belief. A million suns bursting into being each hour—it has been some time since a claim in contemporary philosophy knocked me down like that one did, yet it is no more than the latest sample to have chanced my way. What is hard to realize concretely is that the perennial philosophy upstages the best show science can manage. For without backing off in the slightest on numbers, it makes, as it were, a right-angle turn into a wholly new dimension: that of quality—qualitative experience, we might say, to make sure that it is not abstractions that we are talking about. To see what this involves, we might try to imagine the qualitative difference between the experience of a wood tick and ourselves, and then, continuing on in the same expanding direction, introduce orders of magnitude that science has accustomed us to: 10^{23} or whatever. Or collapse to the size of a drop the degree of reality in the terrestrial plane and then imagine the intermediate plane as an ocean—not oceanically large, but oceanically more real—balanced on top of it, repeating

the operation (intermediate plane reduced to a drop, celestial plane the supervening ocean) until the infinite is reached. If our imaginations could concretely effect such moves we would have no difficulty understanding Plato when he said, "First a shudder runs through me, and then the old awe creeps over me."

To speak of upper planes as more real does not imply that lower ones are unreal or illusory, only less real. Nor does it impugn their worth, for not only does each have its place in the entire scheme; matter anywhere, hosting its master, can become a temple of its Lord. Though I have tried to offset the suspicion that higher and lower on the chain of being involve spatial separation, it may help if we convert the chain into concentric circles with the lower, lesser realms located inside the higher ones in which they "live and move and have their being." Always the less is permeated by the more; the problem is to see this. But it can be seen. "There is no rung of being on which you cannot find the Holiness of being," said Martin Buber. "God's is-ness (*isticheit*) is my is-ness, neither less nor more," said Meister Eckhart. And Hakuin:

> *This earth where we stand is the Pure Lotus Land,*
> *And this very body the body of Buddha*
> ("Chant in Praise of Zazen").

With the metaphysics of the perennial philosophy now before us, the essentials of its psychology and ethics can be dubbed in quickly.

2. PSYCHOLOGY
"The psychology that finds in the soul something similar to, or even identical with, divine Reality." I know of no more efficient way to elucidate Huxley's summary here than through a commentary on the diagram from *Forgotten Truth* on the following page:

In his *Religio Medici* Sir Thomas Browne wrote, "Man is the great amphibian whose nature is disposed to live, not only like other creatures in diverse elements, but in divided and distinguished worlds." These "divided and distinguished worlds" are the multiple levels of reality the preceding section set forth, and in the perennial psychology the human self intersects them all. That they erupt in inverse order, the lesser now appearing above the greater (body above mind, etc.) is appropriate, for microcosm mirrors macrocosm

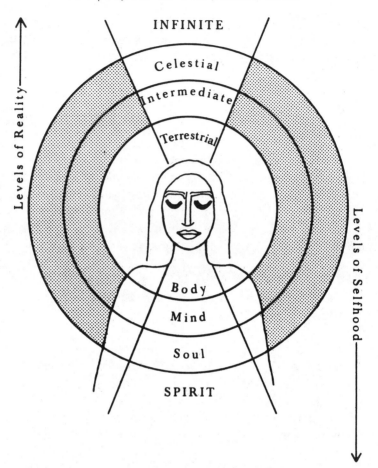

(man mirrors the universe), and mirrors invert. Envisioned externally, the good dons metaphors of height; but when we reverse our gaze and look inward, our value-imagery transposes: it turns over. Within us the best lies deepest; it is basic, fundamental, the ground of our being. The way *body* and *mind* correlate with the terrestrial and intermediate planes is obvious; the former swim, as it were, in the latter. Theists will have no difficulty recognizing the *soul*—final locus of our individuality—as engaged in I-Thou relation with the knowable God. It is the contention that (in Huxley's formulation) there is "in the soul something similar to, or even identical with, divine Reality"—in the diagram this something is named *spirit*— that is most controversial.

The lines of the dispute have, in the course of the centuries, become recognizable. If you persist in walking north, there comes a moment when, though you think you are still headed north, you are actually moving south, for in the preceding step you unwittingly crossed the pole. Theists use this analogy to argue that though mystics think they are entering deeper into God's nature with their notions of spirit and infinite, they are actually departing from the living God who is Lord of history and particularity, community and decision. This is not the place (even were there wish) to argue the mystic's reply to this objection. The issue is rich in subtleties; what, for example, is one to make of Saint Paul's assertion that "the word of God is quick and powerful, and sharper than any two-edged sword, piercing even to *the dividing asunder of soul and spirit*" (Hebrews 4:12, emphasis added; see preceding diagram where soul and spirit are demarcated)? But as the perennial psychology obviously allows an important place for the mystic, reasons must be given for its doing so.

No feature of our nature is more undeniable than its duality: we have a "me" that is circumscribed, and an "I" which, in its awareness of this circumscription gives evidence of being itself exempt from it. The mystic is drawn to this "I"; s-he fixes on it, labors to develop his/her sense of its reality, and generally tries to identify with it as much as possible. And as noncircumscription is its essence, there is nothing that separates it in principle from the infinite. Unconsciously dwelling at our inmost center; beneath the surface shuttlings of our sensations, percepts, and thoughts; wrapped in the envelope of soul (which too is finally porous) is the eternal and the divine, the final Reality: not soul, not personality, but All-Self beyond all selfishness; spirit enwombed in matter and wrapped round with psychic traces. Within every phantom-self dwells this divine; within all creatures incarnate sleeps the Infinite Sentence— unevolved, hidden, unfelt, unknown, yet destined from all eternity to waken at last and, tearing away the ghostly web of sensuous mind, break forever its chrysalis of flesh and pass beyond all space and time.

In the language of the great affirmations, spirit is the Atman that *is* Brahman, the Buddha-nature that appears when our finite selves get out of its way, my *isticheit* (is-ness) which, once we stop standing in our own light, we see is God's is-ness. Back of every wave stands the entire ocean; "the deeper I go within myself, the more I find that which is beyond myself," as Gabriel Marcel said. We catch glimmers of this unbounded "I" in moments when we are so totally engrossed in a task that no attention for our finite self remains—in I/me terms, no "me" appears at all. The need, though, is not to try to anticipate what this desideratum would be like, but rather to see that life's ballast can lodge at any of the four levels of selfhood our diagram depicts; all are present in everyone, but they are actualized to different degrees. In a catalogue that would sound elitist and self-righteous if it were not read as a project for oneself:

> a life that identifies primarily with its physical pleasures and needs ("getting and spending we lay waste our days") is super-ficial;
>
> one that advances its attention to mind can be interesting;
>
> if it moves on to the heart (synonym for soul) in can be good;
>
> and if it passes on to spirit—that saving self-forgetfulness and egalitarianism in which one's personal interests loom no larger than those of others—it would be perfect.

How far life can move in this direction may be left an open question. It is the direction that is pointed, not the distance covered, that counts.

What needs to be added is the epistemological bearing of this "ballast lowering," if we may continue to use this metaphor for the deepening of self that results as its center of gravity settles progressively into the arms of being and becomes more stable in consequence. The perennial epistemology respects reason, but in the way one respects a fine tool; what it accomplishes depends more on who uses it than its own perfection. If it is a power tool, we can visualize outlets on the various levels of being, but now let science fiction enter. The power that increases as the outlets ascend is magical in enabling the tool (reason) to accomplish qualitatively greater marvels as it passes from one to the next; the higher the socket into which reason is plugged, the greater the wonders it can effect. In this somewhat cumbersome image, the outlets represent an intellective capacity that empowers reason and provides the degree of luminosity it enjoys but which must be clearly distinguished *from* reason. Call it the intuitive intellect and see that, while it is always fully present in everyone in the way spirit is—in the end it *is* spirit, but that's a different story—it is actualized to different degrees as the differently powered sockets suggest. If it is not too awkward to join the power-tool image to the earlier one of ontological ballast, the picture that results is as follows: reason plugged in to a life that is fixated on the bodily level will detect little more than matter and will spin a materialistic world view. Things other than matter will be evident to someone who takes his mind seriously, and *his* reason will fashion an outlook that ranges from animism in traditional societies to naturalism in the contemporary West. To those who, their hearts having been opened, can see with *its* eye (the Sufi's "eye of the heart"; Plato's "eye of the soul"), spiritual objects will be discernible and a theistic metaphysics will emerge. The final "night vision" which can detect the awefilled holiness of everything is reserved for those whom, in this essay, I have called mystics.

A section that has already become something of a junk yard for metaphors can stand one more. The divisions between the levels of reality are like one-way mirrors. Looking up, we see only reflections of the level we are on; looking down, the mirrors become plate glass and cease to exist. On the highest plane even the glass is removed, and immanence reigns. To anticipate the sentence that begins the next section: looking up from planes that are lower, God is radically transcendent (*ganz Anders;* wholly other); looking down, from heights that human vision (too) can to varying degrees attain, God is absolutely immanent.

3. ETHIC

"The ethic that places man's final end in the knowledge of the immanent and transcendent Ground of all being."

A few years ago the *Review of Metaphysics* published an essay by Jacob Needleman with the arresting title, "Why Philosophy is Easy." In the past, Needleman noted, philosophy was thought to be anything but easy. Only the ablest citizens were expected to undertake it, and even they, only after training not only their minds but their bodies, their emotions, and their wills as well. This has of course changed. Today everyone is encouraged to try his or her hand at the art, even high school students. The switch has occurred because rational abilities are now considered the only prerequisites. The reason the others have been dropped, Needleman goes on to say, is that the wisdom the modern philosopher seeks through his philosophy is no longer a new state of being. "The abandonment of this [former] objective more than any single conceptualized point of view," he concludes, is what "distinguishes modern philosophy from so much of ancient and medieval philosophy."[12]

The difference becomes apparent when we note the kinds of experience the two philosophies appeal to. Modern philosophy's touchstone is *generic* experience: experiences of perception, linguistic usage, moral decisions, and the like, that are familiar to us all. Because Ernest Gellner is unique in being not only a philosopher in his own right but also a sociologist who studies philosophers and their discipline professionally, I shall refer to his findings more than once in these essays. His report on the present point is that beliefs, if they are to be considered legitimate today, must pass "the empiricist insistence that [they] be judged by . . . something reasonably close to the ordinary notion of experience.'"[13] This comes close to being the exact opposite of philosophy's former goal, which was to realign the components of the soul in ways that would enable it to experience the world in an *un*ordinary way—a way so *extra*ordinary, in fact, that from its perspective, passion-and-ignorance-laden ordinary experience seems almost psychotic. It is the abandonment of this former, exalted objective that makes contemporary philosophy relatively easy.

I have used Needleman's point to introduce this brief section on ethics because it helps us to position that enterprise in the primordial outlook. An ethic is an assemblage of guidelines for effecting the self-transformation that enables the world to be experienced in a new way. In doing so, it is integrally related to anthropology on the one hand and epistemology and ontology on the other: revised, reformed conduct (ethics) leads to a new condition of self (anthropology) which includes as its principal yield the capacity to see and know (epistemology) the world (ontology) more truly as it is.[g]

---

[g] Occasionally we find a modern philosopher echoing this claimed link between ethics and outlook, as in this statement by William James: "Practice may change our theoretical horizon, and this in a two fold way: it may lead into new worlds and secure new powers. Knowledge we could never attain, remaining what we are, may be attainable in consequence of higher powers and a higher life, which we may morally achieve." (Quoted in Aldous Huxley, *Perennial Philosophy*, p. viii.)

There are also Wittgenstein's famous assertions: "The philosopher's treatment . . . is like the treatment of an illness. . . . Sickness . . . is cured by an alteration in the mode of life of human beings. . . . Pretensions are a mortgage which burdens a philosopher's capacity to think." (Compiled from *Philosophical Investigations*, p. 255; *Remarks on the Foundations of Mathematics*, p. 57; and *On Certainty*, p. 549.) Well and good, but what does modern philosophy do with such occasional asides? What is the altered "mode of life" that is intimated? How is it achieved?

As for the content of the primordial ethic, which in *The Abolition of Man* C. S. Lewis refers to as the *Tao,* meaning by that the value system in which the moral imperatives of all the major traditions coalesce, it condenses (in Western idiom) in the virtues of humility, charity, and veracity; alternatively (expressed negatively and in Asian idiom), it focuses on the three poisons that work against those virtues, the poisons being greed, aversion, and ignorance. Humility has nothing to do with low self-esteem. It is the capacity to distance oneself from one's private, separate ego to the point where one can see it objectively and therefore accurately, as counting for one, but not more *than* one, even as charity sees one's neighbor as counting fully *for* one. Both these initial virtues, which pertain to the human order, announce the arrival into that order of the third virtue, veracity—the capacity to see things in what Buddhists call their *suchness;* the way they actually, accurately, objectively *are.* With self and other made interchangeable through this objective, numerical "one," humility is seen as looking on oneself as if one were another (and as severely as truth allows, but not more), while charity is to look on the other as if he were oneself (as indulgently as truth allows, but again not more). These terse pronouncements show that the primordial ethic in no way neglects the interpersonal, but as its attention never strays far from the whole, what comes through most strongly in its ethical discussions is the cosmic alignment that the virtues effect. To pick up again with humility: to be freed of self is to become emptied and hollow; in this hollow, as Annie Dillard says, you catch grace as a man fills his cup under a waterfall. Or to tie the hollowness to sound, for our ears to hear the music of the spheres its amplitude must be raised. We must turn ourselves into resounding songboxes, carving out careful emptinesses like those in cellos and violins.

To return to epistemology, if wisdom, the capacity to see things as they truly are, is a correlate of virtue,[h] it requires methods for *acquiring* that virtue. It is not necessary here to detail those methods, the spiritual exercizes and "eightfold paths" of the various historical traditions; only the general point need be noted. The perennial philosophy is a path to be walked as much as it is a map that charts that

---

[h] "Virtue . . . is necessary, for light does not go through an opaque stone and barely illuminates a black wall; so man must become like crystal or like snow, but without pretending that snow is light" (Frithjof Schuon, *Spiritual Perspectives and Human Facts* [London: Perennial Books, 1969], p. 178).

path. Knowing and doing, wisdom and method, work together; they walk hand in hand. Close from the start, they draw increasingly so, to the point where it becomes difficult to tell them apart. In Marco Pallis's formulation, wisdom comes to look increasingly like static method (counsels as to how to live) and method like dynamic wisdom (the way wisdom would appear were it enacted).

Only one more point remains. Against the current tendency to glorify one's own inner promptings—the state of "Saint Ego" wherein nothing seems quite so wonderful and worth heeding as some aspect of one's own self—the primordial outlook notes that if those promptings were reliable we would be at the end of our journey, not its start. The most useful service they can perform is to guide one to a tradition that contains the winnowed wisdom of a civilization or culture. It is difficult to imagine a verdict that favors that wisdom over private judgment more categorically than this one by my colleague, the social psychologist Donald Campbell—that he arrives at it through scientific considerations only augments its force. "On evolutionary grounds," Campbell writes,

> it is just as rational to follow religious traditions which one does not understand as it is rational to continue breathing air before one understands the role of oxygen in bodily metabolism. If modern psychology and social science disagree with religious tradition on ways of living one should, on rational and scientific grounds, choose the traditional recipes for life for these are the better tested. Priests who narrow the precious tradition which they transmit to that pittance which they themselves can understand and agree with are neglecting their duty and are guilty of hubris or pretension of omniscience.[14]

NOTES

1. New York: Harper and Brothers, 1945, p. vii.
2. Frithjof Schuon, *The Transcendent Unity of Religions* (New York: Harper & Row, 1975), p. 19.
3. *The Degrees of Knowledge* (New York: Charles Scribner's Sons, 1959), p. 59.
4. *Janus: A Summing Up* (New York: Vintage Press, 1979), pp. 289–90.
5. *The Varieties of Religious Experience* (New York: Longmans, Green & Co., 1902).
6. *Some Problems of Philosophy* (New York: Longmans, Green & Co., 1911), p. 101.

7. Quoted in Harold Schilling, *The New Consciousness in Science and Religion* (Philadelphia: United Church Press, 1973), p. 110.

8. Arthur Young, *Which Way Out?* (Berkeley: Robert Briggs Associates, 1980), p. 2.

9. Quoted in Lewis Thomas, "Debating the Unknowable," *Atlantic Monthly,* July 1981, p. 51. See J. E. Lovelock, *Gaia* (Oxford University Press, 1979).

10. "The Limits of Psychiatry," *The Progressive,* May 1967, pp. 32–33.

11. Frithjof Schuon, *Understanding Islam* (Baltimore: Penguin Books, 1972), p. 7.

12. Jacob Needleman, "Why Philosophy Is Easy," *Review of Metaphysics* 22, no. 1 (September 1968): 3–4.

13. *The Legitimation of Belief* (Cambridge: Cambridge University Press, 1974), p. 206.

14. From the prospectus of a seminar on "Social Evolution and the Authority of Religious Tradition."

Part Three

LOOKING AROUND
An Angle on Our Times

When the primordial tradition first jumped seriously to my attention, my mind had evidently reached a stage of saturated solution which needed but the shock of the right contact to recrystallize in forms that were a revelation. The world they brought to view was not categorically different; it was rather that it glistened in sharp focus. When invitations came my way to comment on several aspects of contemporary culture—higher education, the humanities, and theology—I found I now had things that seemed worth saying. The essays that register those thoughts form the third section of this book, beginning with the current state of higher education.

·4·

EXCLUDED KNOWLEDGE
*A Critique of the Modern Western Mind-Set**

> *The learning of the imagination can remain an*
> *excluded knowledge only so long as the premises*
> *of material science remain unquestioned and*
> *their exclusions undetected.*
>
> Kathleen Raine

The editor of this journal has done something unusual. He has invited me to present my thoughts precisely because they "are not shared by most educators today," which is to say not shared by most readers of this journal. I have been eager to get on with some other work, but I find this concern to get at fundamental issues compelling. I shall write in a personal vein because I think that an indication of how I came to the atypical views that have impressed themselves on me will help throw into relief what those views are. And if (beginning with my title) I sound brash and argumentative, I hope the reader will understand that this is to get huge issues into sharp focus in small compass.

I begin with the journey that brought me to where I now am.

I. PRELIMINARIES

My first book chanced to be on education.[a] It was well received. Robert Ulich, perhaps the grand old man of educational philosophy

* Reprinted with permission from *Teachers College Record*, vol. 80, 3 November 1979.
[a] Huston Smith, *The Purposes of Higher Education* (New York: Harper & Brothers, 1955). "Chanced" is the exact word here, for the book almost did not get written. Had I not run into a professor of speech who said he had been meaning to tell me that he was using a committee report I had written in his choral reading class, that report would have remained buried in my

at that time, rated it above the famed 1945 "Redbook," Harvard University's *General Education in a Free Society*.

Thanks to this early and, as the preceding footnote indicates, almost fortuitous venture into educational theory, the professionals in that field seem for twenty years to have considered me one of them—at least I have felt included. When teaching encountered the new medium of television, the American Council on Education asked me to consider the implications.[1] The American Broadcasting Company included me in its 1962 "Meet the Professor" series. I was invited to deliver the 1964 Annual Lecture to The John Dewey Society,[2] and in that same year to assess the state of the humanities for the fiftieth anniversary issue of Liberal Education.[3] When T-groups and "encounter" came along, the National Training Laboratories, an arm of the National Education Association, invited me to Bethel, Maine, to consider the role of group dynamics in the learning process;[4] and when political rumbles broke out on college campuses in the late 1960s, Phi Beta Kappa asked me for an analysis of the traumas Vietnam and other factors were occasioning higher education.[5] I have lost count of the educational conferences I have participated in, but find that at least two produced printed fallout.[6]

I have included these autobiographical paragraphs to make the point that in education theory I have not been an outsider. For the bulk of my career I have been emphatically "in." Why, then, am I now out?—"out," I want to stress, only in that my views have grown atypical, not that my feelings are estranged. The shape of my ideas may have taken a curious turn, but my interests in ideas themselves has never been livelier. I remain a teacher,[b] and I have never doubted that given the vocational slots of the modern world, the university is my home.

As for the content of my thoughts, which (as has been indicated) now run rather counter to the prevailing academic mind-set, they

files until discarded. As it was, the idea of a committee report being intoned as art was so bizarre that I unearthed the document and reread it. It was the report of a committee that had been appointed to define the aims of liberal education at the university where I was then teaching (Washington University, St. Louis), and finding that it did read passably, I dispatched it to a publisher. The reply was back in a week. The contents had to be expanded tenfold, but a contract was enclosed.

[b] I almost wrote "born teacher," for when my father built his children a workshop I lost no time in converting it into a schoolroom. Tools were shelved, benches brought in, and my younger brother and the servants' children—we were in China—impressed for pupils. And I? I assumed the podium as if authorized by the Mandate of Heaven, if not the Tao itself. The sensation has never left me. Imprinting is too weak. It is enough to make one consider reincarnation.

are spelled out in the book that brought the invitation to write this essay. Titled *Forgotten Truth: The Primordial Tradition,* it was published by Harper and Row in 1976; the Colophon paperback appeared a year later. I shall be itemizing the book's key claims and arguing their validity, but before doing so let me enter a final propaedeutic. I want to note how the opposition between truth as I now see it and the prevailing contemporary mind-set broke upon my awareness.

It came into view through the conjunction of two elements that, once I got them sorted out, bounced off each other like antagonists. Even so, they had no choice but to keep on interacting—honing my perceptions of each; getting their outlines into clearer and clearer focus—because both were locked within me. Call the components East and West or past and present, the facts are that I was born and raised in China and sometime later found myself teaching at M.I.T. A more unlikely conjunction of opposites would be difficult to imagine. China (the China of my boyhood at least) represented tradition and the past, whereas M.I.T. stood for "the future in microcosm," as we liked to say. China was religious (folk religion, mostly, but religious all the same), whereas M.I.T. was secular—its chapel has no windows, as if the architect were saying, "No hope for transcendence here unless you blot out the Institute completely." And China was humanistic whereas M.I.T. was scientific.

Pulled in these opposite directions, my fifteen years in Cambridge were tumultuous. They were also exhilarating, absorbing, and above all instructive. As they progressed I discovered, first, an organic connection between the three terms on each side of the divide: optimally defined, it seemed to me, "traditional," "religious," and "humanistic" have more in common than I had realized, as do "modern," "secular," and "scientific." But then came the surprise. I found that if I stayed with the problem instead of capitulating to accepted ways of construing things—giving in to Bacon's "idols of the theater"—there was no way I could avoid the conclusion that truth sides more with the first of these two sets of triumvirates than with the second.

Before I say why that conclusion seemed forced on me, let me introduce the two antagonists—the two contenders for truth—more properly. For simplicity's sake I shall refer to the first triumvirate as tradition and the second as modernity. The gist of their differences is that modernity, spawned essentially by modern science, stresses quantity[c] (in order to get at power and control) whereas tradition stresses quality (and the participation that is control's alternative). That's the nub of the matter, but the assertion is compact, so I shall amplify it.

The point is this. Before the rise of modern science in the seventeenth century, the entire world, humanly speaking,[d] was wrapped in an outlook that had embraced it from its start, the outlook that in the subtitle to *Forgotten Truth* I designate "The Primordial Tradition." I must describe that outlook of course, but let me back into doing so. As it was science that unhorsed tradition, if we understand what science is we shall be on our way toward understanding the soul of the perspective it dislodged.

II. THE NATURE OF SCIENCE

I agree with those who say that science is not one thing, but to conclude that its multiple facets are joined by no more than "family resemblances" gives up the hunt too quickly.[e] There is a discernible thrust to these facets, which this diagram from my book is designed to identify.

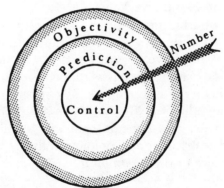

---

[e] Cf. René Guénon. *The Reign of Quantity* (Baltimore, Md.: Penguin Books, 1972), and this statement by Gerald Holton: "The difficulty has perhaps been not that this new way [of separating primary quantifiable properties from secondary qualitative ones] was too hard, but that it turned out to be all too easy. Once the scientists of the seventeenth century had found the key to this particular gate, the road that opened beyond led more speedily and deeply into remote and fascinating territory, further from the original ground of understanding the world" (*Thematic Origins of Scientific Thought* [Cambridge: Harvard University Press, 1973], p. 440).

[d] "Entire" overstates the case slightly, but not much. Mary Douglas tells us in *Natural Symbols* that every type of society, from the most secular to the most religious, can be found in the tribal world, but my point concerns proportions.

[e] A quick review of the signification that led up to the current meaning of our word "science" can help orient us for what follows. *Scientia* in the classical world meant reasoned disclosure of something for the sake of the disclosure itself. Up to the seventeenth century such disclosure consisted largely of classifications of things that were qualitatively different,

No knowledge deserves to be called scientific unless it is objective in the sense of laying claim to intersubjective agreement. Many things meet this initial requirement, however, without being scientific in any rigorous sense—court testimony, for example. We move closer to science proper when we come to truths that enable us to predict[f]—what cannot be falsified is not scientific—and closer still when we reach truths that facilitate control. Each move we make toward the center finds our knowing increasingly locked into mathematics, number being (as is often remarked) the language of science. Numbers lend themselves to the objectivity and precision science seeks because, unlike words, they are unambiguous—more on this later.

The achievements of this thrust toward truth—I am thinking of the noetic achievement of pure science quite as much as the pragmatic achievements of technology—have been so dazzling that they have blinded us to the fact that they are products of an exceedingly restricted kind of knowing. Look what falls outside its ken:

1. Intrinsic and Normative Values

"Values. A terrible business. You can at best stammer when you talk about them," Wittgenstein remarked, illustrating his point by the form of his very utterance. Science can deal with instrumental values but not intrinsic ones. It can tell us that nonsmoking is conducive to health, but whether health is intrinsically better than somatic gratification it cannot adjudicate. Again, it can determine what people do like (descriptive values) but not what they should like (normative values). Market research and opinion polls are sciences but there can be no science of the *summum bonum*.

---

but after Galileo it became the search for nature's quantitative laws. The German *Wissenschaft*, however, continues to carry broader denotations than our English "science" and includes all scholarly disciplines; it is in this German sense, for example, that Marxism claims to be scientific. It is my contention that our English word has come to refer basically to what goes on in the natural or empirical sciences and their mathematical underpinnings. In saying that "physics is a science," no one feels it necessary to warn his hearer that he means that it is a natural science, whereas "sociology is a science" will provoke dispute if the qualifying adjective "social," functioning here as a diminutive, is not added.

[f] B. F. Skinner stands as a parody of the lengths to which science's concern for predictability can drive a man. When it was suggested to him sometime back that it would be a mistake for psychology to take a position on determinism that the Heisenberg Principle had shown to be unsupportable in physics, Skinner replied that the "muddle of physics" was physics' worry, not psychology's. From the fact that electrons are unpredictable, he seemed to be saying, it doesn't follow that human beings are. See T. W. Mann, ed., *Behaviorism and Phenomenology* (Chicago: University of Chicago Press, 1964), pp. 139–40.

2. Purposes

To attribute an intentional character to what happens in nature is anthropomorphic, and anthropomorphic explanations are the opposite of scientific ones. For science to get down to work seriously, Aristotle's final causes had to be banished and the field left free for explanation in terms of efficient causes only. "The cornerstone of scientific method is . . . the *systematic* denial that 'true' knowledge can be got at by interpreting phenomena in terms of final causes— that is to say, of 'purpose.'"[7]

3. Global and Existential Meanings

Science itself is meaningful throughout, but there are two kinds of meaning it cannot get at. One of these is global meanings—what is the meaning of it all? It is as if the scientist were inside a large plastic balloon; he can shine his torch anywhere on the balloon's interior but cannot climb outside the balloon to view it as a whole, see where it is situated, or determine why it was fabricated. The other kind of meaning science cannot handle is existential: it is powerless to force the human mind to find its discoveries meaning*ful*. Let the discovery be as impressive as you please; the knower always has the option to shrug his shoulders and walk away. Having no handle on meanings of these two specific kinds, science "fails in the face of all ultimate questions" (Jaspers) and leaves "the problems of life . . . completely untouched" (Wittgenstein).

4. Quality

This is basic to the lot, for it is their qualitative dimensions that give values, meanings, and purposes their pride of place in life. Yet it is precisely this qualitative dimension that eludes the quantitative measuring grid that science must try, at least, to impose on events if they are to become precise data. Certain qualities (such as tones or colors) are connected with quantifiable substrates (light waves of varying lengths), but quality itself is unmeasurable. Being a subjective experience, it cannot be laid out on a public chopping block; being a simple experience, it cannot be dissected even introspectively. In consequence, it is "refractory to measurement"—not just provisionally, but in principle.

We cannot say that in experience one light has twice the brightness of another. The terms in which we measure experience of a sound are not terms of experience. They are terms of the stimulus, the physical sound, or of the nervous or other bodily action concomitant with the experience. . . . The search . . . for a scale of equivalence between energy and mental experience arrives at none.[8]

Qualities are either perceived for what they are or they are not so perceived, and nothing can convey their nature to anyone who cannot perceive it directly. The most that one can do is to compare things that have a quality with things that do not, and even then the comparison is meaningful only to persons who know from experience what the quality in question is. Science's inability to deal with the qualitatively unmeasurable leaves it dealing with what Lewis Mumford calls a "disqualified universe."

This account of what science cannot deal with is certain to encounter resistance. Not, as far as I have been able to discover, because it is untrue. All that would be required to show that it is untrue would be a counterexample—a single instance in which science has produced precise and provable knowledge concerning a normative value, a final cause, an existential or global meaning, or an intrinsic quality. Considering the importance of these four domains for human life—for three hundred years mankind has all but held its breath waiting for science to close in on them—the fact that it has made no inroads whatever would seem to be a clear sign that science is not fashioned to deal with them. The reason we resist science's limitations is not factual but psychological—we don't want to face up to them. For science is what the modern world believes in. Since it has authored our world, to lose faith in it, as to some extent we must if we admit that its competence is limited, is to lose faith in our kind of world. Such loss of faith would be comparable to the crisis that would have visited the Middle Ages had it suddenly discovered that God was only semicompetent—that he was not God but just another god. The fall of a God is no small matter.

The moves to avoid admitting the limitations of science take two turns. It is argued either that science is not as I depict it; or that it is, but its character will change.

1. *First objection:* Science is not as I depict it. It is more flexible, more human, and more humane than I make it appear.

a. First version: Scientists are as human as the rest of us. Their idealism, warmth, and natural piety—a quotation from Einstein on his mystical feeling for the universe can be expected—is as well developed as the next man's.

Answer: I have said nothing to the contrary. I am talking neither about the persons who discover scientific truths nor about the ends to which their truths are directed—ends that obviously can be either helpful or destructive. I am talking about the character of scientific truth itself.

b. Second version: I make it sound as if there were a single scientific method that delivers discoveries almost on command, whereas in fact that method—insofar as there is a method in the singular—is as "human" as any other. It is human both in the noble sense of pivoting on distinctively human capacities for inspiration and imagination, and in the less noble, "all too human" sense of being subject to pitfalls. Science is fallible. False starts, blind alleys, in-house vendettas, and outright mistakes are conspicuous parts of its record. (Citations from Michael Polanyi, Thomas Kuhn, Abraham Maslow, and James Watson's *The Double Helix.*)

Answer: If the preceding confusion lay in failure to separate scientific truth on the one hand from the persons who discover it and the ends to which it is put on the other, the confusion here lies in conflating such truth with the processes by which it is reached—the psychology and sociology of scientific discovery. The routes by which scientists arrive at their discoveries may be as inspired, diverse, and fallible as one pleases—I personally think Feyerabend's *Against Method* goes too far, but I agree that the scientific method can never be completely formalized. But again, that is not what I am talking about. My eye is not on how science is acquired. It is on the truth its acquisition-process arrives at. Or more precisely, it is on the defining features of such truth—the kind of truth science tries to get at.

c. Third version: I make objectivity the minimum requirement of scientific knowledge just when we are coming to see that there is no such thing.

Answer: Here the confusion is between two meanings of objectivity. Science need not be objective in the sense of claiming to mirror the way things are in themselves—the so-called camera theory of knowledge. One can even go so far as to say that in its frontier reaches science says very little about what nature itself is like;

mostly it tells us how it responds to the experiments we direct toward it, with the result that these experiments must themselves figure in our conclusions as to what has been disclosed. Knowing of this kind is indeed subjective in the sense of conforming to a knowing subject. But this kind of subjectivity does not touch the objectivity science demands as its admissions ticket, which (to repeat) is consensual agreement. Man may be as implicated in his knowing as you please; science asks only that he be implicated generically rather than idiosyncratically—that he be implicated as physicist, say, rather than as Jones or Smith.

2. So much for the first objection, that science is not as I have depicted it. The *second objection* accepts my account as applicable for today's science but not necessarily for tomorrow's.

Answer: Obviously science will change in many respects; the question is: Will its changes be of the sort that enable it to deal with the values, purposes, meanings, and qualities it has thus far neglected? (The change from classical to relativity physics was momentous, but it changed nothing in physics' stance toward the four lacunae I keep citing.) If science is to deal with these lacunae, it will have to relax the demands for objectivity, prediction, control, and number that have excluded it from qualitative domains while producing its power in quantitative ones. We are free, of course, to turn science in this new direction, a direction that is actually old in that it points back to the preseventeenth-century, partly-alchemical notion of what science should be. What we must realize is that every step taken toward humanizing science in the sense of moving it into the four fields it has thus far ignored will be a step away from its effectiveness in the sense of its power-to-control. For it is precisely from the narrowness of its approach that the power of modern science derives. An effective and restricted science or one that is ample but does not enable us to control the course of events much more than do art, religion, or psychotherapy—we can of course define the word as we wish. What is not possible is to have it both ways.

As this issue of the *Record* focuses on values that include religion, this section on science should perhaps be rounded off by noting that the stress I place on the differences between science and religion runs counter to the prevailing trend, which is to accent their similarities, a trend that has led theologians to appreciate Teilhard de Chardin,

Michael Polanyi, and Thomas Kuhn (for all their merits) perhaps extravagantly. I think this bedfellows approach holds dangers. We see, I think, what prompts the approach. If it can be shown that science resembles religion, perhaps the credibility of the first will rub off onto the second. The kicker, however, is this: the similarities that are being made so much of in the current science/religion discussions concern person (the scientist who does science), method (how science is done), or application (the uses to which science is put), none of which, taken individually or even collectively, rival in importance a fourth issue, namely, the kind of knowledge science seeks. Science has advanced to the unrivaled respect it now enjoys by virtue of the kind of knowledge it has discovered and the control to which such knowledge lends itself. It is with reference to this kind of knowledge, therefore, that it deserves to be defined and by our society will be defined—alternative proposals by theologians or philosophers are not going to change this. The result is that any credibility rub off from science onto religion that may derive from associating the two will be outweighed by the pull to conform religious truth to scientific: the more religion is linked with top-dog science, the greater will be the expectation that its truth conform to the top dog's successful mold. The process is subtle but very strong. It is at work in the academic study of religion where objectivity has already become an almost undisputed norm.

III. THE TRADITIONAL, AND IN EFFECT PRIMORDIAL, OUTLOOK

I hope that the preceding section has not cast scientists in the role of white-coated bad guys. I do not know if science has brought more harm or good even to date, much less what the long-term balance will show. Pointing fingers nowhere save at ourselves—at us, denizens of the modern world in general, and even here there is no finger pointing really; we would have had to have been prescient demigods for what has happened not to have happened—I am occupied with a single phenomenon, quite a simple one really. When attention turns toward something it turns away from something else. The triumphs of modern science—all in the material world, remember—have swung our attention toward the world's material aspects. The consequence—could anything be more natural?—has been progressive inattention to certain of the world's other properties. Stop attending to something and first we forget its importance; from there it is only a matter of time till one begins to wonder if it exists at all.[g] But let me invoke another voice to make my point more graphically.

In his posthumous *A Guide for the Perplexed,* a book that appeared a year after *Forgotten Truth* and parallels it to the point that it can be read as the same book for a different audience, E. F. (*Small Is Beautiful*) Schumacher tells of being lost while sight-seeing in Leningrad. He was consulting his pocket map when an interpreter stepped up and offered to help. When he pointed on the map to where they were standing, Schumacher was puzzled. "But these large churches around us, they aren't on the map," he protested. "We don't show churches in our maps," he was informed. "But that's not so," Schumacher persisted. "That church over there—it's on the map." "Oh, that," the guide responded. "That's no longer a church. It's a museum."

Comparably, Schumacher goes on to say, with the philosophical map his Oxford education provided him: Most of the things that most of mankind has considered most important throughout its history didn't show on it. Or if they did, they showed as museum pieces—things people used to believe about the world but believe no longer.

The anecdote provides an ideal entrée to the traditional world view in suggesting that modernity omits something—as the title of my own book puts the matter, it has forgotten something. This something, which constitutes the ontological divide that separates tradition and modernity, is higher realms of being—domains of existence that begin precisely where science stops. "Higher" functions metaphorically here, of course—the additional realms are not spatially removed. But if we discount this literal, spatial sense of higher, they are superior in every (other) way. They are more important. They exert more power. They are less ephemeral. They are more integrated. They are more sentient and therefore more beneficient. And they enjoy more felicity, a felicity that in the highest octaves phases into beatitude. Ontologists fuse these various facets

---

[g] An example at hand: The item I wrote just before starting this present essay was a review of Bollingen's two-volume posthumous compilation of the writings of A. K. Coomaraswamy, so I looked up John Kenneth Galbraith's review of the set in *The New York Times Book Review.* It was delightful, of course, but he dismissed the second volume of the set, which contains Coomaraswamy's metaphysical writings, with a single sentence: "It worries me in stating as true what can only be imagined" (12 March 1978).

of worth by saying that the higher regions have more being. They are more real.

If the reader finds such notions incredible, his response is completely understandable; the truth I have come to think they represent would not be forgotten, again as in *Forgotten Truth,* if they pressed the "of course" button within us. Theodore Roszak voices the typical incredulity of today's intellectual toward the primordial vision when, in reviewing the Schumacher book just alluded to, he writes: "It does no good at all to quote [Aristotle, Dante, and Thomas Aquinas], to celebrate their insight, to adulate their wisdom. Of course they are wise and fine and noble, but they stand on the other side of the abyss" (*Los Angeles Times,* 11 September 1977). But capacity to believe (or disbelieve) has never been a reliable index of whether the belief in question is true; innumerable social, historical, and psychological factors affect what people are able to believe. I do not argue that the primordial vision continues today to seem self-evident or even (to our practical, workaday sensibilities) plausible. What has escaped me, if it is around, is anything modernity has discovered that shows it to be mistaken. In searching for negative evidence I naturally turned first to science, only to find that when its discoveries are freed of interpretations the facts themselves do not require, they slip into the folds of tradition without a ripple. Only when negativism intrudes and the successes of science are wittingly (as in positivism) or unwittingly (as in modernity generally) used to erode confidence in realities other than those science can handle—when, in a phrase, science phases into scientism—does opposition appear. Tradition (a word I try never to pronounce with contempt) incorporates science, whereas scientism excludes tradition by fiat. The fact that tradition has the more generous, inclusive purview stands for me as at least an initial count in its favor.

Were I to say in detail what the higher reaches of reality are, there would be no room to suggest before I close some possibilities they hold for education. So, accenting their primordial, near-universal character, I shall say briefly that in addition to practical life, which is grounded in (1) the material or *terrestrial* plane, every known culture has allowed a place for religion, which, to accommodate important differences in spiritual personality types, proceeds on three levels: folk religion, theism, and mysticism. Folk religion is involved with what Plato calls (2) the *intermediate* plane (*to metaxy*); theism

with (3) the *celestial* plane (Wilhelm Schmidt's "High God," a supreme divinity manifesting personal attributes, classical theism),
and mysticism with (4) the *Infinite*—God in his ineffable mode: the
Tao that cannot be spoken, nirvana, sunyata, and Godhead. "The
Great Truth about the world," as Schumacher says, "is that it is a
hierarchic structure of four great 'Levels of Being.' "[9]

To amplify only slightly:

1. The matrices of the terrestrial plane are space, time, and matter. Science seems to be developing nearly ideal procedures for understanding it. We are so into the scientific way of seeing things that
we tend to think of this physical stratum as foundational; we assume that it could exist without the others, but not vice versa. In
point of fact, however, from our human point of view, matter (primary qualities, "vacuous actuality") is far from our starting
point—it is with experience, not matter, that we begin. Phenomenology has come forward to make this point painstakingly and, as
counterpoise to the reductionism that results when we forget it, is
an important movement.

2. Human life is so obviously psyche and soma, body and mind,
that the terrestrial and intermediate planes are usually best considered together. Nevertheless, the intermediate plane does contain
ingredients that exceed its manifestly human ones that phenomenology attends to. These additional ingredients have the looks
of a hodgepodge, a grab bag—they constitute the world of tarot
cards, tea leaves, and premonitions, as someone has characterized it. The animate denizens of this world are gods, ghosts, and
demons; the "little people" of various description; the "controls" of
spiritualists, mediums, and amanuenses; departed souls in limbo,
purgatory, and the Tibetan bardos—in a phrase, discarnates generally. Some of these are so suspect that I am embarrassed even to list
them, but one man's mush is another man's meaning, so in view of
the difficulty of producing reliable criteria for sorting out what has
at least some factual basis, it is best at this point to be egalitarian. So
much nonsense goes on in the name of this intermediate or psychic
plane that it takes a bit of courage to say, as did both Margaret
Mead and Gregory Bateson, that something does go on. The
courage can be less if we depersonalize the contents of the intermediate plane, for as we have now come to assume that the universe

that wraps us round is by and large impersonal, it is easier for us to countenance forces or entities that fit this description. Regarded as impersonal, the contents of the intermediate plane turn up as psi phenomena of parapsychology, "coincidences" (as in Arthur Koestler's *The Roots of Coincidence*), Jungian archetypes, and astral influences—again, much winnowing is needed to separate the wheat from the chaff. Dreams seem to have some sort of privileged access to this plane, and Theodore Roszak's *Unfinished Animal* is lush witness that interest in it is not confined to traditional cultures or unsophisticated minds in ours. A leading analytic philosopher recently observed that whereas Freudianism has a marvelous theory but no facts, parapsychology has facts but no theory. The second half of his statement holds pretty much for the intermediate plane generally. Enigmatic energies of some kind seem to be at work, but, as we have noted, it is the very mischief to verify them or identify what they are. And let me repeat that it is usually best to think of the terrestrial and intermediate planes together, for on the one hand the terrestrial cries out for infusion from the intermediate to account for the difference between life and nonlife, while the intermediate for its part resembles the terrestrial in being a maelstrom of forces that threaten as much as they sustain us.

3. Impersonally, the celestial plane consists in Western idiom of the Platonic archetypes as integrated in the Idea of the Good. Personally, as we have said, it is the God of classical theism.

4. The Infinite is everything, integrated to the unimaginable point of excluding separations. It can be intuited, but words can depict it only paradoxically, for univocal assertions (being definite) necessarily exclude something, which the Infinite (by definition) cannot.

It bears repeating that the higher planes are not more abstract. Quite the contrary, each ascending plane, in addition to being incredibly vaster, is more concrete, more real, than the ones below. Only on superior levels are the contents of lower levels revisioned to make the way they first appeared seem, like dreams on awakening, relatively unreal. This last phrase, "relatively unreal," should be glossed to read, "not totally unreal, but requiring revision from the way they appear on planes that are more restricted."

The disappearance of the higher planes of reality from our contemporary philosophical maps—or, to speak more carefully, the decline in our confidence in such planes—is, as I say, the change that separates modernity from tradition most decisively.[h] In common parlance, our outlook has become more this-worldly, "this world" being the one that connects with our senses. And it is clear from what I have said that I think the change has impoverished our sense of what the world includes and what it means to be fully human—in giving "ultimate authority to the world view of a slightly sleepy businessman right after lunch," to invoke G. K. Chesterton's wry formulation, we have lost our grip on the innate immensity of our true nature.[i] It stands to reason that a new ethos has emerged to fit this reduced onto-anthropology, and before I turn to saying a thing or two about education I need to dub in that ethos. My sketch holds, I think, for our culture as a whole, but again especially for today's university.

IV. THE ETHOS OF THE MODERN WEST

The most pertinent way to characterize the modern ethos briefly is to say that it is a blend of naturalism and control. The two terms are related, for it is our wish to control that has brought our naturalism. By way of a new epistemology, we can add, so we actually have three things going: our will to power, its attendant epistemology, and the metaphysics this epistemology brings in its train.

1. Promethean Motivation

Can anyone doubt that science has enlarged man's power incalculably,[j] or that this is the primary reason we are so invested in it? Life by its very nature is beset with problems, and problems cry out to be solved. Since science, via technology, is the most effective problem solver we have developed, it is natural that in trying to solve the

---

[h] "If anything characterizes 'modernity,' it is a loss of faith in transcendence, in a reality that encompasses but surpasses our quotidian affairs," we read in "Review of *Facing Up to Modernity* by Peter Berger," *The Chronicle of Higher Education,* 9 January 1978, p. 18. Because this quotation spots the exact phenomenon that prompted the writing of these essays, it will be cited several times in the course of this book.

[i] "We are the only people who think themselves risen from savages; everyone else believes they descended from gods," Marshall Sahlins tells us in *Culture and Practical Reason* (Chicago: University of Chicago Press, 1976). And from Saul Bellow's 1976 Nobel Prize address: "We do not think well of ourselves; we do not think amply about what we are. . . . It is the jet plane in which we commonplace human beings have crossed the Atlantic in four hours that embodies such values as we can claim."

[j] It has also rendered us as a species more vulnerable, but that has only recently come to light.

problems that beset us we have come to look increasingly in science's direction.

This much seems clear. What we are only beginning to see is that Prometheanism breeds a distinctive epistemology.

2. Promethean Epistemology

Let me introduce Ernest Gellner here, for as a philosopher-sociologist who brings his sociological equipment to bear on analyzing philosophy, his conclusions are more than personal opinions; they claim, at least, to report on the conditions of philosophy in general. In his *Legitimation of Belief* he tells us that underlying the seeming variety, choas even, of twentieth-century philosophy, an "emerging consensus" can be discerned. Having for some time accepted that epistemology is philosophy's current central task, philosophers are now coming to agree, broadly speaking, that to be recognized as legitimate, beliefs must pass certain tests. "There is the empiricist insistence that faiths . . . must stand ready to be judged by . . . something reasonably close to the ordinary notion of 'experience'. Second, there is the 'mechanistic' insistence on impersonal . . . explanations."[10]

Without dropping a word, Gellner proceeds to acknowledge that it is our Prometheanism that has established this twofold requirement:

> We have of course no guarantee that the world must be such as to be amenable to such explanations; we can only show that we are constrained to think so. It was Kant's merit to see that this compulsion is in us, not in things. It was Weber's to see that it is historically a specific kind of mind, not human mind as such, which is subject to this compulsion. What it amounts to is in the end simple: if there is to be effective knowledge or explanation at all, it must have this form, for any other kind of "explanation" . . . is *ipso facto* powerless.
>
> We have become habituated to and dependent on effective knowledge, and hence have bound ourselves to this kind of genuine explanation. . . . "Reductionism," the view that everything in the world is really something else, and that something else is coldly impersonal, is simply the ineluctable corollary of effective explanation.[11]

Gellner admits that this epistemology our Prometheanism has forced upon us carries "morally disturbing" consequences:

> It was also Kant's merit to see the inescapable price of this Faustian purchase of real [sic] knowledge. [In delivering] cognitive effectiveness [it] exacts its inherent moral, "dehumanizing" price. . . . The price of real knowledge is that our identities, freedom, norms, are no longer underwritten by our vision and comprehension of things.[12] On the contrary we are doomed to suffer from a tension between cognition and identity.[13]

Even so, Gellner concludes, we must accept this tension, for the only alternative to "effective knowledge" is "meretricious styles of thought" aimed at "restoration of the moral order within a cosy world in which identities and moral norms were linked in a closed circle of definitions."

3. Naturalistic Metaphysics

Given the way Promethean reason imposes itself on the objects it works with, the world it presents to us can be viewed as the product of a vast display of ventriloquism in which the so-called external world is a dummy; if this comparison, which I take from Philip Sherrard, leans too far in the direction of science-as-construct, it at least gets us past the simplistic model of the archeologist who discovers through straightforward acts of uncovering. Empiricism and mechanism being ill suited to deal with transcendence and the unseen, the epistemology of Prometheanism necessarily conjures for us a naturalistic world. Hannah Arendt stressed this toward the close of her life. "What has come to an end," she wrote, "is the . . . distinction between the sensual and the supersensual, together with the notion, at least as old as Parmenides, that whatever is not given to the senses . . . is more real, more truthful, more meaningful than what appears; that it is not just beyond sense perception but above the world of the senses."[14] Emphasizing that "what is 'dead' is not only the localization of . . . 'eternal truths' but the [temporal/ eternal, sensual/supersensual] distinction itself," Dr. Arendt continues with some sentences that are serious enough, perhaps even momentous enough, to be quoted in full:

Meanwhile, in increasingly strident voices, the few defenders of metaphysics have warned us of the danger of nihilism inherent in this development; and although they themselves seldom invoke it, they have an important argument in their favor: it is indeed true that once the supersensual realm is discarded, its opposite, the world of appearances as understood for so many centuries, is also annihilated. The sensual, as still understood by the positivists, cannot survive the death of the supersensual. No one knew this better than Nietzsche who, with his poetic and metaphoric description of the assassination of God in Zarathustra, has caused so much confusion in these matters. In a significant passage in *The Twilight of Idols,* he clarifies what the word God meant in Zarathustra. It was merely a symbol for the supersensual realm as understood by metaphysics; he now uses instead of God the word true world and says: "We have abolished the true world. What has remained? The apparent one perhaps? Oh no! With the true world we have also abolished the apparent one."[15]

V. IMPORT FOR EDUCATION

Education has so much to learn. It needs to learn, needs to see, what is happening to it, and what it should do in the face of this happening.

What is happening to it is that it is being pressed increasingly into the service of the kind of knowing that facilitates control. Inasmuch as our will-to-control has cut our consciousness to fit its needs—tailored our awareness to fit its imperatives—our educational attempts naturally conform to this tailoring. I shall not attempt to document this assertion systematically—only to note a few straws in the wind.

Philosophy

The place where philosophy intersects science is of course logic, and the growth of logical concern in twentieth-century philosophy has been dramatic. It is going too far to suggest, as someone recently has, that philosophy departments have in effect now become departments of applied logic, but the trend to "do philosophy" via the formal arguments of symbolic logic is unmistakable. Even in the philosophy of language, Chomsky's mildly metaphysical (Cartesian) interests are being overtaken by Donald Davidson's effort's to apply symbolic logic to natural languages. The other side of the coin is, of course, the "melancholy, long, withdrawing roar" of philosophy's retreat from metaphysics; where world views cannot be avoided entirely, the species that is usually admitted is a brand of mechanism, materialism, or empiricism—a recent *New York Times* report refers to "the materialism that is overwhelmingly predominant in current analytic philosophy."[16] Yet neither Quine nor Kripke—the senior and junior "Mr. Logics" of our time—think that empiricism or materialism are themselves empirically grounded.[17] They have been instated—I am speaking for myself now—because they are the premises that support most forthrightly the kind of knowledge that facilitates control.[18]

Economics
"Contemporary economics thinks of itself as a science, heavily quantitative, using mathematics and statistics as its vocabulary. Paul Samuelson and Wassily Leontief are its giants."[19] In *Small Is Beautiful,* E. F. Schumacher contends that its quantitative orientation has become so excessive, so totally devoid of qualitative understanding, that even the quality of "orders of magnitude" ceases to be appreciated.

Political Science
"The profound option of mainstream social scientists for the empiricist conception of knowledge and science makes it inevitable that they should accept the verification model of political science," Charles Taylor, Professor of Social and Political Theory at Oxford University, tells us. "The basic premise [of this approach is] that social reality is made up of brute data alone," data that is objective in requiring no interpretation and being in principle recordable by machines. The consequence, Professor Taylor concludes, is that a "whole level of study of our civilization . . . is ruled out. Rather [it] is made invisible."[20]

History
A member of the external examining committee that was appointed a year or two back to review the graduate history program at my university happened to belong to the new breed of quantitative

historians. At one point in the committee's deliberations he was reported to have said, "If you can't count it, you might as well be playing football." Granted that his statement was extreme, it says something about our times that a responsible academic could have said it at all.

Anthropology
"English-speaking anthropology over the last half century has been and continues to be passionately scientistic in its hopes and claims, and methods. One consequence—and it shares this trait with other sciences—is a built-in positivism and an aversion to history, both general and its own."[21]

Psychology
Insofar as there is a model of man in academic psychology, it seems still to be basically Freudian, and "classical psychoanalytic theory is based quite explicitly on a specific, highly materialist view of man's nature."[22]

The Social Sciences Generally
Charles Taylor generalizes the point we quoted him as making about political science as follows:

> The progress of natural science has lent great credibility to this [verificationist] epistemology, since it can be plausibly reconstructed on this model. . . . And, of course, the temptation has been overwhelming to reconstruct the sciences of man on the same model; or rather to launch them in lines of inquiry that fit this paradigm, since they are constantly said to be in their "infancy." Psychology, where an earlier vogue of behaviorism is being replaced by a boom of computer-based models, is far from the only case.[23]

May Brodbeck notes that there are

> two factors within the social disciplines. One of them exuberantly embraces the scientific idea; the other [introducing the distinction between *Verstehen* and explanation], exalts its own intuitive understanding as being superior in logic and in principle to scientific explanation,[24]

but Thomas Lawson of Western Michigan University says that recent scholarly critiques of the nonscientific faction have "been so powerful and penetrating that [it is] bankrupt."[25] This seems to justify the following overview in the September 1978 issue of *The Atlantic Monthly*:

> The social sciences are, or aspire to be, sciences; they have a scientific methodology. . . . The majority of social sciences have adopted a form of radical empiricism. According to this doctrine, the only sentences that are scientifically acceptable are those that are directly verifiable by experiment. . . .
>
> This methodology was borrowed from the teachings of the logical positivists. . . . Logical positivism was given up long ago by most scientists and philosophers, including many of the positivists themselves. Yet this positivistic doctrine . . . has taken firm root in the social sciences. It has done so because it provides a simple (if oversimple) distinction between fact and value which allows social scientists to make the (sometimes bogus) claim of scientific objectivity.[26]

The Arts

I shall let the poet Kathleen Raine describe the situation here.

> Poets of the imagination write of the soul, of intellectual beauty, of the living spirit of the world. What does such work communicate to readers who do not believe in the soul, in the spirit of life, or in anything that can be (unless the physically desirable) called "the beautiful"? For in René Guénon's "reign of quantity" such terms of quality become . . . "meaningless," because there is nothing for which they stand. . . .
>
> What can be saved from a culture whose premises are of a spiritual order in an iron age peopled by Plato's "men of clay" (the human primate of the scientist) is the quantifiable; the mechanics of construction, in whatever art. And the engineering element in the making of a poem is negligible in comparison with that of the most impressive and typical work of the reign of quantity, the space-ship. What meaning is there, in materialist terms, to the word "poet"; or the essence—the "poetry"—and the quality—the "poetic"—of works of art?[27]

Geography

I save for last a field that shows some signs of a turning tide. Following World War II, geography's classic concern with place lost ground to a more abstract, geometric concern for space; a recent issue of the *Canadian Geographer* refers to "a generation of geographical treatment of the man-environment relationship as a measurable, objective, and mechanistic entity which may be examined through concepts and methods derived from the natural sciences." It goes on, however, to place the "high tide of [this] scientific geography in the last decade," the 1970s having shown signs of "a fundamental dissatisfaction with positivist philosophies of social science and the perceived implications of such study for our social and geographical world."[28] The geographers at my own university tell me the empiricist school must still be reckoned the dominant one, but in this field there seem to be signs of a "rise of soul against intellect," as Yeats would put the matter.[29]

I have mentioned only a handful of disciplines, and even in these have done little more than report some straws in the winds that have blown my way since I started to think about this essay. If they add up to no more than a straw man, there may be no problem. But if they are accurate in suggesting that the academic mind is leaning excessively toward the scientific model, what is to be done?

If it is true, as I have argued:

> first, that the exceptional power-to-control that modern science has made possible has made us reach out insistently, perhaps even desperately if we feel we are on a treadmill, for ever-increasing control;

> second, that this outreach has forged a new epistemology wherein knowledge that facilitates control and the devices for getting at such knowledge are honored to the neglect of their alternatives;

> and third, that this utilitarian epistemology has constricted our view of the way things are, including what it means to be fully human;

if, as I say, these contentions are essentially accurate, it behooves us to decide if we want to change our direction, and if so, what a better direction might be.

On the first question, it is obvious from the tenor of my entire essay that I think we can do better than continue down our present path. The main reason I would prefer an alternative is that I think that with respect to things that matter most our present course is taking us away from truth more than toward it, but there is a supporting reason. There are reports that life in the cave we have entered does not feel very good. As I do not trust my own intuitions here—they could easily be self-serving—I shall let a colleague, who as a sociologist studies societies directly, make the point.

> It is by now a Sunday-supplement commonplace that the social, economic and technological modernization of the world is accompanied by a spiritual malaise that has come to be called alienation. At its most fundamental level, the diagnosis of alienation is based on the view that modernization forces upon us a world that, although baptized as real by science, is denuded of all humanly recognizable qualities; beauty and ugliness, love and hate, passion and fulfillment, salvation and damnation. It is not, of course, being claimed that such matters are not part of the existential realities of human life. It is rather that the scientific world view makes it illegitimate to speak of them as being "objectively" part of the world, forcing us instead to define such evaluation and such emotional experience as "merely subjective" projections of people's inner lives.
>
> The world, once an "enchanted garden," to use Max Weber's memorable phrase, has now become disenchanted, deprived of purpose and direction, bereft—in these senses—of life itself. All that which is allegedly basic to the specifically human status in nature, comes to be forced back upon the precincts of the "subjective" which, in turn, is pushed by the modern scientific view ever more into the province of dreams and illusions.[30]

If we have trimmed our epistemological sails too close to the scientific desiderata of objectivity, prediction, number, and control (see diagram on p. 65), and it is this that has constricted our world view and brought alienation, it seems only sensible to consider alternative guidelines—perhaps even opposite ones to get the matter in sharp relief. The alternatives to objectivity, prediction, control, and number are subjectivity, surprise, surrender, and words. With the exception of the last of these four terms, it sounds odd even to suggests that education might turn toward them. This shows how deeply committed we are to the scientific quartet; the question is, are we too deeply implicated with it even to imagine what an education that swung toward the neglected alternatives would look like?

Subjective education would recognize that it is as important to understand oneself as one's world or its parts. It would distinguish between objective and subjective (existential) truths, the latter being defined as truths we acknowledge not only with our minds but with our lives as well—we live as if we really do believe that they are true. And it would argue that "truth" deserves the prefix "subjective" as much as the prefix "objective."

Education for *surprise* would begin with, and keep always in full view, its indisputable premise: in comparison with what we do not know, what we do know is nothing. Balancing our present assumption that education's role is to transmit what we know, education for surprise would not reject that premise but would add that it is equally important to remember how much we do not know. Learning theory? Who knows, really, how we learn? Medicine? I go to visit my neighbor Robert Becker at New York's Upstate Medical Center because of interesting things I have heard about his research and he greets me with, "We know nothing!" "Welcome to the club," I reply, having studied the skeptical tradition in Western philosophy rather thoroughly. "That's not what I mean," he says. "It may be true generally, but it's especially true in medicine. Here I am, a director of medical research with thirty years behind me, and when I cut my face shaving I haven't any idea what makes it heal." Generalizing Becker's point, education for surprise would remind students that the more we know, the more we see how much we do not know. The larger the island of knowledge, the longer the shoreline of wonder. Noting that neither language nor science is rule-directed in the sense of proceeding by the application of rules we can discern and explicitly state, it would pay special attention to case studies where the long shot carried the day. It might even try to hone students' sensibilities to surprise by asking questions like, "Did anything surprise you yesterday?" On the flyleaves of the training manuals for such education we might paste this statement, titled "The Strangest Age," from *Newsweek,* 25 July 1977:

> Perhaps ours is the strangest age. It is an age without a sense of the strangeness of things. . . .
>
> The human race has grown up and lost its capacity for wonder. This is not because people understand their everyday world better than people did in earlier ages. Today people understand less and less of the social and scientific systems on which they depend more and more. Alas, growing up usually means growing immune to astonishment. As G. K. Chesterton wrote, very young children do not need fairy tales because "mere life is interesting enough. A child of 7 is excited by being told that Tommy opened the door and saw a dragon. But a child of 3 is excited by being told that Tommy opened the door." The 3-year-old is the realist. No one really knows how Tommy does it.

Education for *surrender* sounds strangest of all, not only because of the military associations of that word but because it runs counter to the penchant that has created our modern world. Recognizing that it would be working against some of our strongest social instincts, such education would remind us that life proceeds by breathing out and in, giving and receiving, doing and being, left hemisphere and right, yang and yin; moreover, too much imbalance between the poles can make life capsize. It would show that only in the realm of things—the realm I have called the terrestrial plane—are freedom and the control to which it can be put attractive even as ideals; the last thing a man in love wants to hear from his beloved is that he is free, while to enter a friendship or marriage with intent to control is to sully it from the start. In life's higher reaches, freedom and the will-to-power are symptoms of detachment in its pathological sense of inability to cathect. To be unable to give oneself—to a person, a cause, the call of conscience, God, something—is to lack a capacity that is integral to being fully human. It is to be incapable of commitment. Kurt Wolff says that "the seminal meaning of 'surrender' is 'cognitive love,'" and notes certain other meanings that "follow from it: total involvement, suspension of received notions, pertinence of everything, identification, and risk of being hurt."[31] Heidegger's continuing influence on our campuses in the face of his tortuous language and unpopular premises derives in part, at least, from the sense that there is something inherently right in the *Gelassenheit* toward which his philosophy points. Someone has translated *Gelassenheit* as "reverent, choiceless letting-be of what is in order that it may reveal itself in the essence of its being."

Reading, writing, and arithmetic: Education is always involved with words, but in opposing them to numbers I am focusing on a specific feature. Words are symbols, whereas numbers are only signs.[32] Because signs are univocal, they can lock together in logics that compel assent, but this cannot be said of symbols, which are multivalent in principle. Their inbuilt ambiguity makes logicians flee them for univocal signs,[k] but humanists prize their equivocality. A biologist has stated their case succinctly:

> Ambiguity seems to be an essential, indispensable element for the transfer of information from one place to another by words, where matters of real importance are concerned. It is often necessary, for meaning to come through, that there be an almost vague sense of strangeness and askewness. Speechless animals and cells cannot do this. . . . Only the human mind is designed to work in this way, programmed to drift away in the presence of locked-on information, straying from each point in a hunt for a better, different point.[33]

Language is biological in that we are programmed to learn it, Dr. Thomas concludes, but it is peculiar in being a "programming for ambiguity." An education-for-words that is alert to their symbolic virtues would teach that the need to be clear must not be allowed to sterilize language—rid it of the humus of adumbration and allusion that makes it fertile and capable of reaching into every crevice of the human soul. The point is crucial for dilating our sense of world. We cannot go back to very old civilizations where words virtually doubled for things by borrowing their full substance, but there is no reason why we cannot come again to see that at its best symbolism is the "science" of the relationship between alternate levels of reality (al-Ghazali).

The foregoing has deduced the outlines of an alternative education by reversing the criteria of scientific knowing. I might have gotten to much the same place if I had asked what education would

---

[k] Paul Ricoeur points out the irony in the phrase "symbolic logic" which, as the name for our ultimate, formal, abstract exacitude, exactly inverts the symbolism's usual meaning (*The Symbolism of Evil,* trans. Emerson Buchanan [Boston: Beacon Press, 1969], p. 17).

look like if it attended more to the things science is not skillful with: intrinsic and normative values, purposes, existential and inclusive meanings, and qualities. But I have said enough for today, save for a quick coda.

I hope what I have written has not contributed to the literature of indictment. I have tried, or hope I have tried, merely, to ask myself where we are and where it might be good to go. The second half of this question, "Where might it be good to go," does not, I think, implicate me in the homilist's complaint of living in bad times, but it does bring my argument full circle in a way I had not anticipated. Going is a mode of doing, and doing includes an element of control. But the will-to-control, having caused our narrowed epistemology and ontology, is what we need to correct—this has been my argument.

The paradox—recommendations issuing from one side of a mouth that preaches *wu wei* (nonwillfullness, noninsistence) with its other side—could be embarrassing were it not in fact a virtue. For it shows that at least we have not been wrestling with a straw man. If motivations (intentions) do breed their respective epistemologies and worlds and it has been our historical destiny to push the problem-solving triumvirate to dangerous extremes, the question remains: What is the right balance between participation and control? I do not know the answer. If I were a university president forced to divide short funds between knowledge that furthers participation and knowledge that furthers control, I would agonize. Everything I have written is premised on the intuition that we are top-heavy on control, but those who disagree are powerful and worthy of the utmost respect and even fear. So much so that I shall ask Gregory Bateson to address to them my final rejoinder. His statement appears in an interview with Daniel Goleman in *Psychology Today*.

GOLEMAN: What's to be done?

BATESON: Funny question, "What's to be done?" Suppose I said that nothing's to be done. Way back in 1947, I was asked to address a group of physicists at Princeton. They had all worked on the atom bomb, and then were terribly remorseful about what might be done with it. Robert Oppenheimer had organized a seminar for these nuclear physicists to examine the social sciences to see if there were any remedies. After my talk, I was Oppenheimer's house-guest. The next morning was a horrible, rainy winter day. The children had lost their rubbers and Mrs. Oppenheimer was going mad trying to get them off to school. The regular American breakfast scene.

And in the midst of all this hubbub, out of the blue, came the still, small voice of Oppenheimer, saying, unasked, "You know, if anyone asked me why I left teaching at Cal Tech and came to do research at Princeton, I suppose the answer was that at Cal Tech there were 500 students to face, who all wanted to know the answers."

I said, "I suppose the answers to these questions would have been rather bitter."

Oppenheimer said, "Well, as I see it, the world is moving in the direction of hell, with a high velocity, and perhaps a positive acceleration, and a positive rate of change of acceleration; and the only condition under which it might not reach its destination is that we and the Russians be willing to let it go there." Every move we make in fear of the next war in fact hastens it. The old deterrence theory. We arm up to control the Russians, they do the same. Anxiety, in fact, brings about the thing it fears, creates its own disaster.

GOLEMAN: So, just let it happen?

BATESON: Well, be bloody careful about the politics you play to control it. You don't know the total pattern; for all you know, you could create the next horror by trying to fix up a present one.

GOLEMAN: The patterns you talk about in which we are enmeshed seem much larger than we can grasp.

BATESON: There is a larger mind of which the individual mind is only a subsystem. This larger mind is perhaps what some people mean by "God." But it is immanent in the total interconnected social system and includes the planetary ecology.

GOLEMAN: It seems to be almost futile to try to perceive, let alone control, this larger web of patterns and connections.

BATESON: Trying to perceive them is, I'm sure, worthwhile. I've devoted my life to that proposition. Trying to tell other people about them is worthwhile. In a sense, we know it already. At the same time, we don't know. We are terribly full of screaming voices that talk administrative "common sense."

GOLEMAN: Rather than. . .

BATESON: Wisdom. If there be such a thing.[34]

NOTES

1. Huston Smith, "Teaching to a Camera," *Educational Record,* January 1956.

2. Expanded, it was published as Huston Smith, *Condemned to Meaning* (New York: Harper & Row, 1965).

3. Huston Smith, "The Humanities and Man's Condition," *Liberal Education* 50, no. 2 (May 1964).

4. Huston Smith, "Two Kinds of Teaching," in Thomas Buxton and Keith Prichard, *Excellence in University Teaching* (Columbia, S.C.: University of South Carolina Press, 1975); reprinted in *Key Reporter* 38, no. 4 (Summer 1973), and in *Journal of Humanistic Psychology* 15, no. 4 (Fall 1975).

5. Huston Smith, "Like It Is: The University Today," *Key Reporter* 34, no. 2 (Winter 1968–1969). Reprinted in *Wall Street Journal,* 20 March 1969.

6. Huston Smith, "Values: Academic and Human," in *The Larger Learning,* ed. Marjorie Carpenter (Dubuque, Iowa: William C. Brown, 1969); and Huston Smith, "Education beyond the Facts," (Charleston, W.V.: Morris Harvey College, 1962).

7. Jacques Monod, *Chance and Necessity* (New York: Random House, 1972), p. 21.

8. Sir Charles Sherrington, *Man on His Nature* (Cambridge: Cambridge University Press, 1963), p. 251.

9. E. F. Schumacher, *A Guide for the Perplexed* (New York: Harper & Row, 1977), p. 8.

10. Ernest Gellner, *The Legitimation of Belief* (Cambridge: Cambridge University Press, 1975), p. 206.

11. Ibid., pp. 206–7.

12. Sartre's "absurd" is a corollary of the positivism that denies any essential meaning that is not empirically verifiable.

13. Ibid., p. 207.

14. Hannah Arendt, "Thinking and Moral Consideration," *Social Research* 38 (Autumn 1971): 240.

15. Ibid.

16. Taylor Branch, "New Frontiers in American Philosophy," *New York Times Magazine,* 14 August 1978.

17. Quine sees ontological positions—what is finally real—as relative precisely because they cannot be objectively grounded, and Kripke has written as follows: "Materialism, I think, must hold that a physical description of the world is a complete description of it, that any mental facts are 'ontologically dependent' on physical facts in the straightforward sense of following from them by necessity. No identity theorists [materialists] seems to me to have made a convincing argument against the intuitive view that this is not the case." (closing section of his paper "Naming and Necessity").

18. For the reason why persons who are seeking "effective knowledge" (Gellner's phrase) are required to charge persons who work from alternative metaphysical premises with "begging the question," see my discussion of D. C. Dennett's work in *Forgotten Truth: The Primordial Tradition* (New York: Harper & Row, 1976), pp. 135ff.

19. Adam Smith, *New York Times Book Review,* 18 September 1977, p. 10.

20. Charles Taylor, "Interpretation and the Sciences of Man," in *Understanding and Social Inquiry,* ed. Fred Dallmayr and Thomas McCarthy (South Bend, Ind.: University of Notre Dame Press, 1977), p. 124.

21. Robert Ackerman, "J. G. Frazer Revisited," *American Scholar*, Spring 1978, p. 232.

22. Irving Yalom, *The Theory and Practice of Group Psychotherapy* (New York: Basic Books, 1975), p. 85.

23. Taylor, "Interpretation and the Sciences of Man," pp. 105–6.

24. May Brodbeck, ed., *Readings in the Philosophy of the Social Sciences* (New York: Macmillan, 1968), p. 2 of the "General Introduction."

25. Thomas Lawson, unpublished paper, 1974.

26. Alston Chase, "Skipping through College: Reflections on the Decline of Liberal Arts Education," *The Atlantic Monthly*, September 1978, p. 38.

27. Kathleen Raine, "Premises and Poetry," *Sophia Perennis* 3, no. 2 (Autumn 1977): 58–60.

28. *Canadian Geographer* 22, no. 1 (Spring 1978): 66–67.

29. As this article goes to press, something has come to my attention that suggests that philosophy, which in a sense is epistemology's custodian, may itself be starting to recover from the unautonomous way it has related to science thus far in this century. In *Reason, Truth and History* (Cambridge University Press, 1981), Hilary Putnam, chairman of the Philosophy Department at Harvard, argues: (1) that it is time for philosophy to lay aside the debunking posture that has characterized it for the last fifty years; (2) that the materialism that virtually *is* its current metaphysics and the empiricism that is its epistemology are both inadequate; (3) that its biggest present job is to develop a model of rationality more adequate than the three present contenders—inductive logic, relativism, and innate ideas a la Chomsky; and (4) this new model should be one that establishes philosophy as a cognitive domain situated between science on the one hand and art on the other.

And Richard Rorty, in what may be the most important philosophical work of the decade, *Philosophy and the Mirror of Nature* (Princeton University Press, 1979), asks philosophers to renounce their claim to being authorities on epistemology. Instead, they should turn to the hermeneutic task of facilitating conversation between different worlds of discourse.

30. Manfred Stanley, "Beyond Progress: Three Post-Political Futures," in *Images of the Future*, ed. Robert Bundy (Buffalo: Prometheus Books, 1976), pp. 115–16.

31. Kurt Wolff, "Surrender, and Autonomy and Community," *Humanitas* 1, no. 2 (Fall 1965): 177. See also his "Surrender as a Response to Our Crisis," *Journal of Humanistic Psychology* 2 (1962): 16–30; and *Surrender and Catch* (Netherlands: D. Reidel, 1976).

32. Numerology is a special case that need not concern us here. In 2 + 2 = 4 numbers function as signs, but in "God is one," one is a symbol.

33. Lewis Thomas, *Lives of a Cell* (Toronto: Bantam Books, 1974), p. 111.

34. Gregory Bateson, interviewed by Daniel Goleman, "Breaking Out of the Double Bind," *Psychology Today*, August 1978, p. 51.

·5·

FLAKES OF FIRE,
HANDFULS OF LIGHT
The Humanities as
Uncontrolled Experiment*

This essay continues the theme of the preceding one and relates it specifically to the humanities. It was originally delivered as an address that
formed a part of the week-long festival, "In Celebration of the
Humanities," that marked the move of Syracuse University's humanities
division into new quarters in the autumn of 1979.

T hose of us who saw "Einstein's Universe," that remarkable
television program the British Broadcasting Company created
for the centennial of Einstein's birth, remember the words that laced
it like a theme: "Einstein would have wanted us to say it in the
simplest possible way. Space tells matter how to move; matter tells
space how to warp." How, in the simplest possible way, can we
describe the burden and promise of the humanities today?

1. THE HUMANITIES

First, by identifying their central concern. They have many facets, of
course, but we will not be far from the mark if we think of them as

---

* Reprinted from *Teachers College Record* 82, no. 2 (Winter 1980), and the British review
Temenos 1, no. 2 (1982).

custodians of the human image;[a] one way or another, in cycles and epicycles, they circle the question of who we take ourselves to be— what it means to be a human being, to live a human life. We know that self-images are important, for endowed as we are with self-consciousness, we draw portraits of ourselves and then fashion our lives to their likenesses, coming to resemble the portraits we draw. Psychologists who are professionally concerned with behavior modification tell us that a revised self-image is the most important single factor in human change. It is when a person sees himself differently that new ways of behaving come to seem feasible and appropriate.

If then (in company with religion and the arts in our culture at large) the humanities are custodians of the human self-image, what is their burden and promise today?

II. BURDENS: SOCIAL AND CONCEPTUAL

Turning first to their burdens, they are of two kinds, social and conceptual. As the first of these stems from our culture's institutional forms I shall let a social scientist, a colleague, Manfred Stanley, tell the story. "It is by now a Sunday-supplement commonplace," he writes, "that the social, economic and technological modernization of the world is accompanied by a spiritual malaise that has come to be called alienation."[b] The social changes contributing to this alienation reduce most importantly, I suspect—I am not attributing this further point to Professor Stanley—to disruption of the primary communities in which life used to be lived. No longer rooted in such communities, our lives are seen less in their entirety, as wholes, by others; and in consequence (so fully are our perceptions of ourselves governed by others' perceptions of us) we have difficulty seeing *ourselves* as wholes. High mobility decrees that our associates know only limited time segments of our lives—childhood, college, mid-life career, retirement—while the compartmentaliza-

---

[a] I have decided not to assume a double gender vocabulary, adding "woman" every time I write "man." I shall rely on the reader to understand that I consciously use "man" in the generic sense in which it appears in "human" or "the humanities." While speaking of genders, I should mention my indebtedness to Kendra Smith. It was in company and conversation with her that many of the ideas in this essay emerged or took final shape.

[b] There are two fairly extended quotations which, because they speak so precisely to the points they make, I use more than once in these essays which were written for different audiences. That by Ernest Gellner, which puts its finger on our current epistemology, is one of these; it appeared in the preceding essay and will reappear in this one. The other, which identifies the consequences of that epistemology, is this present statement by Manfred Stanley, which appeared on p. 84 above and will continue on p. 94.

tion of industrial life insures that at any given life stage our associates will know us in only one of our roles; worker, member of the family, civic associate, or friend. Once again, none knows us whole, and as our fellows do not so know us, we have trouble seeing ourselves as wholes as well.

This scattering of our lives in time and their splintering in space tends to fragment our self-image and in extreme cases to pulverize it. Engendering Robert Lifton's "protean man" and abetting the existentialist's conclusion that we have no essence, the disruption of the primary community is, as I say, the heaviest burden I see institutional changes laying on our efforts to see ourselves as complete persons. But the conceptual problem our age has wrought is, if anything, even weightier. By this conceptual problem I mean the world view the modern West has settled into: its notion of "the scheme of things entire" as it finally is. The statement by Professor Stanley that I began quoting speaks to this conceptual side of our predicament too—so precisely, in fact, that I shall continue to let him speak for me. He was noting, you will recall, the alienation that modernization has occasioned, and having alluded to some of its social causes drives straight to the heart of the matter as follows:

> At its most fundamental level, the diagnosis of alienation is based on the view that modernization forces upon us a world that, although baptized as real by science, is denuded of all humanly recognizable qualities; beauty and ugliness, love and hate, passion and fulfillment, salvation and damnation. It is not, of course, being claimed that such matters are not part of the existential realities of human life. It is rather that the scientific world view makes it illegitimate to speak of them as being "objectively" part of the world, forcing us instead to define such evaluation and such emotional experience as "merely subjective" projections of people's inner lives.
>
> The world, once an "enchanted garden," to use Max Weber's memorable phrase, has now become disenchanted, deprived of purpose and direction, bereft—in these senses—of life itself. All that which is allegedly basic to the specifically human status in nature comes to be forced back upon the precincts of the "subjective" which, in turn, is pushed by the modern scientific view ever more into the province of dreams and illusions.

To say that it is difficult—burdensome—to maintain a respectable image of man in a world like this is an understatement. The truth is, it is impossible.[c] If modern man feels alienated from this world he sees enveloping him, it shows that his wits are still intact. He should feel alienated. For no permanent standoff between self and world is possible; eventually there will be a showdown. And when it comes, there is no doubt about the outcome: the world will win—for a starter, it is bigger than we are. So a meaningful life is not finally possible in a meaningless world. It is provisionally possible—there can be a temporary standoff between self and world—but finally it is not possible.[d] Either the garden is indeed disenchanted, in which case the humanities deserve to be on the defensive, no noble image being possible in an a-noble—I do not say ignoble—world; or the garden remains enchanted and the humanities should help make this fact known.

To set out to reverse the metaphysical momentum of the last four hundred years might seem a task so difficult as to be daunting, but there is another way to look at the matter. Here, surely, is something worth doing, a project to elicit the best that is within us, including resources we might not know we possess; so even if we fail in the attempt we shall do so knowing the joy that comes from noble doings. To get the project underway we must advance into enemy territory—we shall find it to be a contemporary form of what Plato called "upside down existence"—and to do this we must cross a no-man's-land of methodology, "no-man's" being precise here because if either side were to capture it the victory would be theirs. So, a short interlude on method to establish the ground rules for the "war of the worlds" (read "war of the world views") we are about to begin.

---

[c] Christopher Lasch gives us one indication of this in *The Culture of Narcissism* which has as its subtitle, *American Life in an Age of Diminishing Expectations*. Saul Bellow's assessment was quoted on p. 76 above and another Nobel Prize winner, the neuro-physiologist John Eccles, has this to say: Man is not just "a hastily made-over ape. . . . Science has gone too far in breaking down our belief in our spiritual greatness" (*Brain/Mind Bulletin,* 20 February 1978, p. 4).

[d] A certain metaphysical sensitivity is needed to see this—a talent for the long view—but the point must rest here with an analogy. From their beginning stars struggle against the force of their own gravity, which they can oppose only by generating tremendous amounts of energy to maintain high internal pressures. But the star can never win the battle, for when its fuel is exhausted, gravity wins and the star must die.

III. METHODOLOGICAL INTERLUDE

In a university setting, any move to reinstate the enchanted garden will naturally be met by the question, "How do you know it is enchanted?" If we answer that we experience it so, that we find ourselves ravished by its mystery and washed by its beauty and presences—not always, of course, but enough to sustain conviction[e]—we shall be told that this is not to know, it is merely to feel. This crude response requires of us a choice. Either we blow the whistle at once on this cramped and positivistic definition of knowledge (as we shall soon see, its willingness to dignify as knowledge only such kinds as hold the promise of augmenting our power to control rules out the very possibility of knowing things that might be superior to us, it being possible to control only subordinates or at most equals; in a word, it rules out the possibility of knowing transcendence) or we can let this restriction of knowledge to what-can-be-proved stand, in which case knowledge becomes a foundation (one among several) for a higher epistemic yield—call it insight, wisdom, understanding, or even intelligence if we use that word to include, as it did for the Scholastics, Plato's "eye of the soul" that can discern spiritual objects. What we must never, never do is make proof our master. Fear that if we do not subject ourselves to it we may wander into error will always tempt us to this slavery,[f] but to yield to the temptation spells disaster for our discipline. Even physicists, if they be great ones, see (as Richard Feynman pointed out in his Nobel Lecture) that "a very great deal more truth can become known than can be proven." "Not to prove, but to discover"[g] must be the humanities' watchword.

To rise above the tyranny of proof and with pounding heart bid farewell to the world of the inadequate—the rope is cut, the bird is free—is in no wise to abandon thoughts for feelings, as if bogs could accommodate the human spirit better than cages. To relegate the health of our souls to the whims of our emotions would be absurd. To say that in outdistancing proof we take our minds with us is too

---

[e] In Alvin Plantinga, *God and Other Minds* (Ithaca, N.Y.: Cornell University Press, 1967), Plantinga says he does not know how to argue the existence of God, whose existence seems as obvious to him as anything he might try to argue it from.

[f] "I am so afraid of error that I keep hurling myself into the arms of doubt rather than into the arms of truth" (Petrarch).

[g] Epigraph of Carolly Erickson's *The Medieval Vision* (New York: Oxford University Press, 1976).

weak; they empower our flight. At this higher altitude the mind is, if anything, more alive than before.[h] In supreme instances the muses take over and our minds go on "automatic pilot," that inspired, ecstatic state Plato called "the higher madness." We cannot here track them to those heights where myth and poetry conspire with revelation and rememberance, science joining them at those times when hunches strike terror in the heart, so fine is the line between inspired madness and the kind that disintegrates. Such ozone atmosphere is not for this essay. Ours is the *to metaxy,* the intermediate realm between proofs that cannot tell us whether the garden is enchanted or not and inspiration that shows us, face to face, that it is. Proofs being unavailable in this "middle kingdom," there remains the possibility that reasons may have something to say—proofs, no; reasons, yes. Even here we should not expect too much, for the more we try to make our reasons resemble proofs—in justifications or arguments that compel provided only that the hearer has rational faculties—the more they must take on proof's earthbound character; in grounding them in demonstrations that compel, we will "ground" them in the correlative sense of preventing them from getting off the ground.

This last point is worth dwelling on for a paragraph, for it points to a dilemma the university is caught in but does not clearly see. On the one hand, we take it for granted that an important part of our job is to train people to think critically; concurrently, we assume that the university is an important custodian of civilization: we have the celebrated retort of the Oxford don who, asked what he was doing for the Battle of Britain, replied that he was what the fighting was *for*. What the university does not see is that the criteria for critical thinking it has adopted work against the high image of man that keeps civilizations vital: the Aryans who fanned out in the second millenium B.C.E. to spread the Indo-European language base from India to Ireland—Aryurvedic medicine still flourishes in India, and Eyre is simply Aryur spelled differently—called themselves

---

[h] "Insight is an act, permeated by intense passion, that makes possible great clarity in the sense that it perceives and dissolves subtle but strong emotional, social, linguistic, and intellectual pressures tending to hold the mind in rigid grooves and fixed compartments, in which fundamental challenges are avoided. From this germ can unfold a further perception that includes new orders and forms of reason that are expressed in the medium of thought and language" (David Bohm, "On Insight and its Significance for Science, Education, and Values," *Teachers College Record* 80, no. 3 [1979]: 409).

Aryan (noble), while the Muslims who entered history in the greatest political explosion the world has known were powered for that explosion by the Quranic assurance, "Surely We created man in the best stature" (XCV, 4). To cite but a single evidence of the contradiction the university is caught in here, "There is no doubt that in developed societies education has contributed to the decline of religious belief";[1] yet students of evolution tell us that "religious behaviors are . . . probably adaptive; [their] dialog with 'nature' . . . is an important integrator of [man's] whole self-view in relation to the world and to activity."[2] I suspect that the conjunction of these two facts—religion is adaptive and the canons of modernity erode it—contributed to Max Weber's pessimism about the future, a pessimism shared by the foremost contemporary British sociologist of religion, Bryan Wilson. Seeing current society as less legitimated than any previous social order, Wilson fears a breakdown of civilizing values in the face of an increasingly anonymous and rationalized culture.[3] I think we should ask ourselves very seriously whether the canons of critical thinking the university has drifted into actually further such a possible breakdown. It has been America's hope that these canons make for a better, more "rational" world. It seems to be her experience that they do not necessarily do so.

But to proceed. If our first methodological point noted that attempts to force the question of the world's worth into the arena of proof preclude a heartening answer by that move alone, the second point concerns an innuendo that must be anticipated and dismissed so discussion can proceed on a decent level. I refer to the charge, more frequently insinuated than openly expressed, that affirmative world views are products of wishful thinking. What are put forward as good reasons to support them are not the real reasons. The real reasons are psychological.

At risk of protesting too much, I propose to raise a small electrical storm here to clear the atmosphere. As barometer to show that the storm is needed, I shall refer to the British philosopher and sociologist Ernest Gellner. In his *Legitimation of Belief* he proposes that only such knowledge as lends itself to "public formulation and repeatability" be considered "real knowledge." He admits that the "moral, 'dehumanizing' price" of this move is high, for it leads to the conclusion that "our identities, freedom, norms, are no longer underwritten by our vision and comprehension of things, [so] we are doomed to suffer from a tension between cognition and identity"—note the enchantment departing the garden like helium from a punctured balloon. But we should pay this price manfully, Gellner contends, for its alternative is "styles of thought [that are] cheap, . . . cosy [and] meretricious." It is rhetoric like this that demands a storm to dispatch it. Gellner does not argue that the kind of knowledge he baptizes as "real" in fact is so; only that "we have become habituated to and dependent on" such knowledge and so "are constrained" to define knowledge this way. "It was Kant's merit," he acknowledges, "to see that this compulsion is in us, not in things. It was Weber's to see that it is historically a specific kind of mind, not mind as such, which is subject to this compulsion."[4] But if anyone questions the worth of this compulsion to which "we have become . . . bound" and proposes to try to loosen its hold on us, he must face, atop this already demanding task, Gellner's insults. For to take exception to his delimitation of "real knowledge" is, to repeat his charge, to engage in "styles of thought [that are] cheap and meretricious." That last word drove me to my dictionary; I wanted to discover with precision how my mind works. According to the *Oxford English Dictionary* it is "showily attractive . . . befitting a harlot."

I deplore this whole descent into name calling. Unworthy of discussions in a university setting, it leaves a bad taste in my mouth; part of me feels petty for allowing myself to have been drawn into it. But the phenomenon is real, so it must be dealt with. Volumes could be assembled of so-called arguments of this kind where a psychologically angled vocabulary is used without apparently taking into account the effect this is likely to have on uncritical minds. Though this kind of language is doubtless not intended to degrade the humanities, it does nevertheless betray an artless style of thinking of its authors. For if "real knowledge" is restricted to what is public and repeatable, what is left for the humanities is mostly unreal knowledge or no knowledge at all.

I hope we are agreed that ad hominem arguments get us nowhere. Naturally, I wonder from time to time if my high regard for life and the world is fathered by desire and mothered by need, but this is a shoe that fits either foot. Psychologists tell us that people give themselves on average more grief through too poor estimates of themselves than through inflated estimates; it is self-contempt, not pride, that we have basically to deal with. So if we insist on playing this psychologizing game perhaps we should invite our prophets of the human nadir to join us on the psychiatrist's couch—Beckett, who admits he was born depressed; Camus, Sartre, whoever your list includes—to see if Diane Keaton in *Manhattan* was right in seeing their gloomy worlds as personal neuroses inflated to cosmic proportions.[i] Wittgenstein once remarked that the world of a happy man is a happy world.

The storm is on its way out, but a last, receding clap of thunder as it makes its departure. When the question of whether we are saved by grace or self-effort became an issue in Japanese Buddhist thought, a militant advocate of self-power (Nichiren) made a statement that was counterdependent to a degree worthy of Fritz Perls. Personal responsibility being everything, he argued, a single supplication for help from the Buddhas was enough to send a man to hell. To which a member of the other-power school replied that as he was undoubtedly destined for hell anyway, being totally incapable of saving himself, he might as well take his supplications along with him as comforts. I confess that, taste for taste, I find this latter posture more appealing than that of existentialists who strut life's stage, histrionically hurling their Byronic defiance—"there's no meaning but my meaning; that which each of us personally creates"—at an unhearing universe; Ernest Becker is the latest culture hero in this existentialist camp. And I can say why I find this latter group less appealing; this switch from the psychologizing and subjectivism I have allowed myself to be dragged into in this discussion to a reason is sign that the storm is over. The existentialists are more self-centered—so, at least, their writings come through to me. In countering the mechanistic image of man that science produced, existentialism arose precisely to recall us to ourselves, to remind us of our individuality and freedom—properties that science cannot deal with. In making this correlation it served an important function; we humanists stand greatly in its debt. But there was something it did not see—probably could not see at mid-century. In countering science's push for uniformities and determining forces it uncritically accepted a third scientific premise, the man/world divide that Des-

---

[i] "Despair is, theologically considered, not only a sin but the greatest of sins: and yet at the same time there is a sort of pride in it, a pleasure even, as in the only great thing left to us. It is also a kind of revenge on those whom we imagine have driven us to it" (Kathleen Raine).

cartes and Newton first moved into place. This third premise no more describes the actual nature of things than do the first two; all three are science's working principles, no more, no less. This uncritical acceptance of the third working principle of science drove the existentialists into an alienated, embattled, egocentric depiction of the human condition. In mistaking the separate, self-contained part of us for our true part, existentialism made a fatal mistake that has confused and lowered our self-estimate. I use the past tense in speaking of it because increasingly it has a passé flavor. It lingers on because theology and humanistic psychology have not gathered the academic strength to replace it with a convincing alternative, and philosophy has not given them enough help in their efforts.

So we come to our central question, asking not if an image of man loftier than either science or the existentialists have given us is possible in our times—that would again divert us to a psychological question, this time the question of whether Western civilization still has the vitality to believe great things. Instead, we ask whether this loftier image is true. Even here, though, we have not reached the bottom line, for as we noted earlier the final question is not whether man is noble but whether reality is noble, it being impossible to answer the first question affirmatively unless the second is so answered.[j] If it be asked why I do not produce a moral culprit for our reduced self-image (evil men who have ground that image into the dust by exploiting us) or even a social culprit (what hope for man in an age of mechanization and technique?), the answer is that important as these tyrannies are, they are not our final problem. Our final adversary is the notion of a lifeless universe as the context in which life and thought are set, one which without our presence in it would have been judged inferior to ourselves. Could we but shake off our anodynes for a moment we would see that nothing could be more terrible than the condition of spirits in a supposedly lifeless and indifferent universe—Newton's great mechanism of time, space, and inanimate forces operating automatically or by chance. Spirits in such a context are like saplings without water; their organs shrivel. Not that there has been ill intent in turning holyland into wasteland, garden into desert; just disastrous consequences unforeseen. So we must pick up anew Blake's Bow of Burning Gold to support "the

---

[j] "Plato understood that all attempts to form a nobler type of man—i.e., all *paideai* and all culture—merge into the problem of the nature of the divine" (Werner Jaeger).

rise of soul against intellect" (Yeats) as intellect has come to be narrowly perceived. To continue with Yeats, this time paraphrasing him, we must hammer loud upon the wall till truth at last obeys our call. We must produce some reasons.

IV. LEAVING THE WASTELAND

Aimed not at individuals (scientists, say) or disciplines (science or the social sciences) but at habits of thought that encroach on us all in the modern West—"there never was a war that was not inward" (Marianne Moore)—the reasons are of two sorts, positive and negative. As the negative reasons mesh better with current styles of thought—what we currently take to be reasonable—I shall begin with them. They are negative because they say nothing about what reality is like; they merely show that the claim that it is a lifeless mechanism has not a rational leg to stand on. My latest book, *Forgotten Truth,* and essay, "Excluded Knowledge," work out this exposé in some detail; here I can only summarize their combined argument.

1. We begin with *motivations.* Nothing is more uncompromising about ourselves than that we are creatures that want.

2. These wants give rise to *epistemologies.* From the welter of impressions and surmises that course through our streams of consciousness we register, firm up, and take to be true those that stay in place and support us like stepping stones in getting us where we want to go. In the seventeenth century Western man stumbled on a specialized way of knowing that we call the scientific method, a packet of directives counseling, first, what we should attend to, and then what we should do with the objects that come into focus through this attention. This new epistemological probe dramatically increased our understanding of how nature works and our control over it.[k] As we welcomed this increase, we "went with" this way of knowing, enshrining it as the supreme way of getting at truth, and what it discloses as truth itself.

---

[k] It was the corridors of power that yawned before Bacon and his cohorts in the seventeenth century that made science so heady. Forming their Invisible College, they divided power into three kinds. Power over themselves science did not seem to offer. Power over others it did dangle, but in the imperialism and colonialism it foreshadowed there seemed to be moral ambiguities, so they scratched this topic from their agenda. It was power over nature that excited them as the unqualified good science was deeding to man.

3. Epistemologies in turn produce *ontologies*—they create world views. In the case in question, the epistemology we fashioned to enlarge our cognitive bite into the natural world produced an ontology that made nature central. It may not be accurate to call this new ontology materialism, but clearly it is naturalistic. Everything that exists must have a foothold in nature (space, time, and matter), and in the end it must be subject to that footing.

4. Finally, ontologies generate *anthropologies*. Man being by definition a part of reality, his nature must obviously conform to what reality is. So a naturalistic world view produces, perforce, a humanistic view of man, "humanistic" being used here as adjective not for the humanities but for a specific doctrine that makes embodied man, man's measure.

So far have we ventured down the road to this Promethean epistemology, naturalistic ontology, and humanistic anthropology that it is virtually impossible for us to see how arbitrary the entire outlook is—how like a barren moonscape it would have appeared to our ancestors and continues to appear to everyone but ourselves. My own birth and early experience in China may make it easier for me to see Weber's point, earlier referred to, that the way our Western minds work is not the way human minds must work; but nothing turns on this. I think we can say that the negative way of making our case for the humanities—our point that rationality in no way requires us to think that the garden is not enchanted—has objective standing. We can argue with those who question it.

V. ENTERING THE HOLY LAND

Not so with reasons we may adduce for thinking that the garden is enchanted. These positive reasons are not illogical, but whether we admit the fact grudgingly or glory in it, the fact itself remains: these positive reasons require, as their premises, so to speak, sensibilities that are unevenly distributed and cultivated. So purely rational clout cannot be expected of them.[1] But as the Buddha said to Mara the Tempter when the latter tried to persuade him not to bother to teach because there was no hope that others could fathom his cul-

---

[1] A scientist has written that whatever we consider ultimate reality to be, one of the reasons we find it to be mysterious and awe inspiring is precisely "its failure to present itself as the perfect and articulate consequence of rational thought" (Henry Marganau in Paul Schilpp, *Albert Einstein: Philosopher-Scientist* [New York: Harper Torchbooks, 1959], p. 250).

minating insight: "There will be some who will understand." So I shall continue. Over the entrance to the magic lantern show in Hermann Hesse's *Steppenwolf* was inscribed, "Not for Everybody." The following four arguments will seem like such only to those who at some level of their being have not been permitted to forget the immensity of what it means to be truly human.

1. *The argument from the human majority.* No culture save our own has disjoined man from his world, life from what is presumed to be nonlife, in the alienating way we have. As Gilbert Durand has pointed out,

> the traditional image of man does not distinguish, nor even want to distinguish, the I from the Not-I, the world from man; whereas the entire teaching of modern Western civilization . . . strives to cut the world off from man, to separate the "I think" from what is thought. Dualism is the great "schizomorphic" structure of Western intelligence.[5]

Laurens van der Post tells of the South African bushmen that wherever they go, they feel themselves known, hence at home. There is no threat, no horror of emptiness or strangeness, only familiarity in a friendly, living environment, hence also the absence of any feeling of loneliness.[6] One of my favorite possessions is a *kakimono* that was given to me by a Japanese friend. In four Chinese characters that are bold and beautiful it proclaims that heaven and earth are pervaded with sentience, infused with feeling. This "majority rule" argument that I am beginning with must naturally face the suspicion that attends all reasonings to the effect that "fifty million Frenchmen can't be wrong." But unless the minority (in this case ourselves) can show reasons for thinking the majority is mistaken (and in this case such reasons do not exist: that was the gist of my negative formulation of the case for the humanities), it seems wise to side with the majority. From within Western parochialism the view that man is of a piece with his habitat may look like it belongs to "the childhood of the human race." Freed from that parochialism it looks like man's central surmise when the full range of human experience is legitimated and pondered profoundly: the view that is normal to the human condition because consonant with the complete complement of human sensibilities.

2. *The argument from science.* We must be careful here, for science cannot take a single step toward proving transcendence. But because it does prove things in its own domain and that domain has turned out to be impressive in its own right, science has become the most powerful symbol for transcendence our age affords. I shall list three teachings of contemporary science that carry powerful overtones for those with ears to hear.

a. Fred Hoyle tells us that "no literary imagination could have invented a story one-hundredth part as fantastic as the sober facts that [science has] unearthed."[7] That reality has turned out to be quantitatively more extravagant than we had supposed suggests that its qualitative features may be equally beyond our usual suppositions. If the universe is spatially unbounded, perhaps it is limitless in worth as well.

b. Wholeness, integration, at-one-ment—the concept of unity is vital to the humanities; it is not going too far to cite radical disunity (the man/world split as a final disjunction) as the fiction that has reduced the humanities to their present low condition. Yet science has found nature to be unified to a degree that, again, we would not have surmised without its proofs. Matter and energy are one. Time and space are one, time being space's fourth dimension. Space and gravity are one: the latter is simply space's curvature. And in the end matter and its space-time field are one; what appears to us as a material body is nothing but a center of space-time's deformation. Once again: If we could be taken backstage into the spiritual recesses of reality in the way physics has taken us into its physical recesses, might we not find harmony hidden there as well—earth joined to heaven, man walking with God?

c. The Cartesian/Newtonian paradigm will not work for quantum physics. It is going to be very difficult to fashion an alternative, for the new physics is so strange that we will never be able to visualize it or describe it consistently in ordinary language. But this is itself exciting. We do not know where we are headed, but at least the door of the prison that alienated us and produced the Age of Anxiety is now sprung. It is true that we do not know where we are going, but scientists themselves are beginning to suggest that our haven may be nowhere in the space-time manifold since that manifold is itself derivative and relative. Our final move may be into a different dimension of reality entirely. David Bohm calls this dimension "the implicate order," an order to which Bell's theorem, Chew's

S-matrix bootstrap model as Fritjof Capra interprets it, and Karl Pribram's holographic model of mind all seem (in their various ways) to point.

3. *The argument from human health.* "Pascal's wager" and James' "will to believe" have made their place in philosophy by virtue of their sensible suggestions as to how to proceed in the face of uncertainty. I propose that we add to them what might be called "the argument from human health." I shall use something John Findlay has written about Hegel to make my point here, replacing his references to Hegel with phrases that describe life's final matrix—in this essay what I have been calling, with Weber, life's garden.

> In my not infrequent moods of exaltation I certainly sense my garden to be enchanted. When I do hard theoretical work and succeed in communicating its results to others, I feel that the whole sense of the world lies in endeavours such as mine, that this is the whole justification of its countless atrocious irritants. I feel clear that the world has sense, and that no philosophy that sees it as disenchanted can express this sense satisfactorily. But in my more frequent mood of mild depression I do not see the world thus. I see it as bereft of sense, and I submit masochistically to its senselessness, even taking more comfort in its cold credibility than in the rational desirability of an enchanted existence. I am not even convinced that there is one best or right perspective in which the world should be viewed: it seems a provocative staircase figure always idly altering its perspective.[8]

The point is this: "depression" and "masochism" are pathological terms. To cast our lot with them, assuming that we see most clearly when we are unwell rather than well, is itself a pathological move. The healthy move, it would seem, is to ground our outlooks in our noblest intuitions. This leads to my fourth and final consideration.

4. *The argument from special insights.* End meets beginning: I come at my close to my title. The title of William Golding's novel *Free Fall* has obvious affinities with my subtitle, "The Humanities as Uncontrolled Experiment," but it is an account its hero gives of something that happens to him in the course of that story that gives me my title proper. Samuel Mountjoy—his name itself elicits a small gasp in the context of the burden and promise of the humanities—is

in a Nazi concentration camp awaiting questioning about plans for a prison break. Frenetically he rehearses the tortures that are sure to be inflicted on him to extract the scrap of information he possesses when suddenly, in his own words, "I was visited by a flake of fire, miraculous and pentecostal; and fire transmuted me, once and forever."[9]

Intimations like these come, and when they do we do not know whether the happiness they bring is the rarest or the commonest thing on earth, for in all earthly things we find it, give it, and receive it, but cannot hold onto it. When it comes, it seems in no way strange to be so happy, but in retrospect we wonder how such gold of Eden could have been ours. The human opportunity, always beckoning but never in this life reached, is to stabilize that gold; to let such flakes of fire turn us into "handfuls of light." This second image comes from a tradition in Islam that reads, "God took a handful of His light, and said to it 'Be Muhammad.'" In its esoteric, Sufic reading, the Muhammad here referred to is the Logos, the Universal Man, the Image of God that is in us all; our essence that awaits release.

NOTES

1. Edward Norman, *Christianity and the World Order* (New York: Oxford University Press, 1979), p. 6.

2. Alex Comfort, *I and That* (New York: Crown Publishers, 1979), pp. 69–70. It is not likely that this estimate of religion's importance, coming as it does from the author of *The Joy of Sex*, is skewed by excess piety.

3. Bryan Wilson, *Contemporary Transformations of Religion* (Oxford: Clarendon Press, 1976), p. 100.

4. Ernest Gellner, *The Legitimation of Belief* (Cambridge: Cambridge University Press, 1975), pp. 206–7.

5. Gilbert Durand, "On the Disfiguration of the Image of Man in the West," monograph published by Golgonooza Press, Ipswich, 1977.

6. Laurens van der Post, *The Heart of the Hunter* (Baltimore, Penguin, 1965), p. 188.

7. Fred Hoyle, *The Nature of the Universe* (New York: New American Library, 1950), p. 120.

8. John Findlay, in Alasdair MacIntyre, ed., *Hegel* (South Bend: Ind.: University of Notre Dame Press, 1976), pp. 19–20.

9. New York: Harcourt, Brace, 1960, p. 188.

·6·

SCIENCE AND THEOLOGY
*The Unstable Detente**

From higher education (our intellectual frontier), through its most value-laden region (the humanities), to God the source of it all—the essays in this section ascend in the regions they examine. As loss of transcendence and the sense of the sacred is one of the Post-Modern Mind's defining features, sight naturally has to labor more as the eye ascends: one must look more intently, as in unfamiliar territory. As the two preceding essays emphasized, the central energies of the West have moved steadily into science and technology, a relentless spirit of rational inquiry aimed at control. One important consequence of this was already evident in the ninteenth century: not only religion but art were moving to the margins. Hegel spoke of both together when he said that, however splendid the gods look in modern works of art, whatever dignity and perfection we might find in the images of God the Father and the Virgin Mary, it is of no use: we no longer bend our knees. "It is a long time," Saul Bellow adds in his Nobel Laureate Lecture, "since the knees were bent in piety."

A. THESIS

Against the prevailing assumption that "the warfare between science and theology" (to resurrect W. E. H. Lecky's phrase) is a thing of the past, I propose to argue that if this is true it can only be because science has won the war. Only an exhausted theology, one about to sink into the sands of science like a spent wave, could fail to sense the enormous tension between its claims and those of a scientific world view.

---

* Reprinted with permission and negligible modifications from *The Anglican Theological Review* 63, no. 4 (October 1981).

There is, of course, a sense in which no tension exists or ever has existed. As truth is one and religion and science are both concerned with it, in principle they must be partners. But that is principle only—de jure, not de facto. For the partnership to work we would need to see clearly the inherent limitations of science and keep them in sharp focus. But we do not see these limitations, largely (I suspect) because we don't want to. Because science augments our power and possessions, we would like to think that it has no cutoff point; that its present limitations are provisional only, and that in time it will break out of them to service our complete selves in the way it now services our bodies. So we encourage it to expand, and count on its doing so. Mostly we want its technological fallout, but we want its theory too. For science derives from the controlled experiment, and as that is as close to proof as we can get, a scientific world view would be one we could wholeheartedly believe. It would be true.

It happens, though, that a scientific world view is impossible. I do not mean that we are a long way from having such a view; I mean that we never will have one—it is impossible in principle, a contradiction in terms. For "world" implies whole and science deals with part, an identifiable part of the whole that can be shown to be part only—most of this paper will be devoted to this showing. Again, it is crucial to see that this is not a temporary limitation but one that is built into science's very nature. To hope for a world view from science is like hoping that increasingly detailed maps of Illinois will eventually produce the ultimate map of the United States.

Three times before I have walked up to this point, approaching it from different directions to try to see precisely where the boundaries of science lie. Here I propose to pull these sallies together—that the *OED* defines "sally" as "rush of besieged upon besiegers" makes the word poetically exact. But because I shall be riding this issue hard, devoting most of my space to it, I should say why I see the limits of science as at once the most important point we need to be straight on in relating science to theology, and concomitantly the one we have yet to see clearly.

It seems to be agreed that a defining feature of modernity is loss of transcendence. The sense of the sacred has declined; phrases like "the death of God" and "eclipse of God" would have been inconceivable in earlier days. I assume that readers of this journal will agree, in addition, that this is a real *loss*; fading of the belief that we live in an ordered universe which is related to other, unseen realms of order in a total harmony cannot but have serious consequences. That people now believe less in theologies generally is one thing,[a] but we must note too that the content of the theologies they are now offered has been diluted. It has been toned down to fit better with our prevailing, largely secular, mind-set.

This last is the most controversial point I shall make, and it may be mistaken though I do not think so. As section three of this essay will be devoted to it, I hurry on here to ask: If our age *is* theologically on the defensive, what drove it into the corner? Many things, one can assume, but it seems clear to me—so clear that I won't even argue the point here—that its chief assailant has been modern science. Science has spawned an outlook whose chief features are *naturalism* (the view that nothing that lacks a material component exists, and that in what does exist it is its physical component that has the final say), *evolution* (generalized as the belief that the more derives exhaustively from the less, the higher from the lower), and *progress* (the centering of hope on a this-worldly, historical future). If we match these planks against the platform that issues from revelation, we get the following lineup:

Epistemology:	Science (the scientific method)	Revelation
Ontology:	naturalism	supernaturalism (transcendence)
Efficient cause:	evolution	creation
Final cause:	progress	salvation

Were we mentally capable of keeping the left-hand column in its place there would be no problem, but the triumphs of science have been too impressive to allow this. Method has mushroomed into metaphysics, science into scientism, the latter defined as the drawing of conclusions from science that do not logically follow. I do not charge this against science, nor its votaries whom I regard with a blend of gratitude, affection, and awe. Scientism is a mark of our times, one we are all victims of and responsible for: in Descartes's

---

[a] "There is no doubt that in developed societies education has contributed to the decline of religious belief" (Edward Norman, *Christianity and the World Order* (New York: Oxford University Press, 1979), p. 6.

fall, we sinned all. As there is no space here to trace its workings piecemeal, I propose to strike at the root. Through the three demonstrations of science's limitations I have alluded to, I hope to expose the delusion that our prevailing, predominantly secular outlook is scientific by showing that no inclusive outlook can be such. If my strategy succeeds, it will show that theology need cater to our prevailing styles of thought only if it wishes to. Nothing in the way of evidence requires that it do so.

II. THE LIMITS OF SCIENCE

A. First Demonstration

In *Forgotten Truth* I noted that though science is not monolithic, its distinctive way of getting at truth—the scientific method—gives it a defining thrust. No knowledge deserves to be called scientific unless it is objective in the sense of laying claim to intersubjective agreement, but we move closer to science proper when we discover truths that enable us to predict, and closer still when we reach truths that facilitate control. Each move we make along this line finds our knowing meshing increasingly with mathematics, number being (as we say) the language of science.[b]

The achievements of this probe for truth have been so dazzling that they have blinded us to the fact that they proceed from an extremely restricted kind of knowing. There are four things science cannot get its hands on.[c]

1. *Intrinsic and Normative Values*

Science can deal with instrumental values, but not intrinsic ones. It can tell us that smoking damages health, but whether health is better than somatic gratification it cannot adjudicate. Again, it can determine what people *do* like, but not what they should like. Opinion polls and market research are sciences, but there cannot be a science of the *summum bonum*.

2. *Purposes*

Science must concede purposes to human beings, and by inference perhaps to other animals as well, but it must try to explain these in

---

[b] This model is presented diagramatically on p. 65 above.
[c] They were noted in the essay "Excluded Knowledge," but are repeated here in slightly different form.

terms of things that originate without purpose; behaviorism is so intuitively improbable that it would have gotten nowhere were it not the most scientific approach to human behavior. To introduce intentions into explanations is anthropomorphic, and anthropomorphic explanations are the opposite of scientific ones. Francis Bacon said this early on. "Teleological explanations in science are the province of theology, not science," he wrote. "They are like virgins dedicated to God, and therefore barren of empirical fruit for the good of man."[1] His point has stayed in place. "The cornerstone of scientific method is . . . the *systematic* denial that 'true' knowledge can be got at by interpreting phenomena in terms of final causes—that is to say, of 'purposes.'"[2]

3. *Ultimate and Existential Meanings*

Science is meaningful throughout, but there are two kinds of meanings it cannot handle. One of these is ultimate meanings (what is the meaning of it all?[d]), while the other type is existential (the kind we have in mind when we say something is meaningful). There is no way science can force the human mind to find its discoveries involving; the hearer always has the option to shrug his shoulders and walk away. Unable to deal with these two kinds of meanings, science "fails in the face of all ultimate questions" (Jaspers) and leaves "the problems of life . . . completely untouched" (Wittgenstein). "Only questions which cannot be answered with scientific precision have any real significance" (E. F. Schumacher).

4. *Quality*

This is fundamental, for it is their qualitative components that make values, meanings, and purposes important. But qualities, being subjective, barely lend themselves to even the minimum requirement of science—objectivity—let alone submit to quantification. Certain qualities (such as colors or sounds) have quantifiable substrates (electromagnetic waves of varying lengths), but quality itself is unmeasurable. Euphrometers have been attempted, but without success, for two pains do not add up to one that is twice as painful, and half a happiness makes no sense. Science's inability to deal with the

---

[d] A laser is splendid for cutting; useless for putting things together. Science has something of this character.

qualitatively unmeasurable leaves it working with what Lewis Mumford calls a "disqualified universe."

This account of what science cannot deal with is resisted, but not, I feel sure, because it is untrue. Given the importance of normative values, final causes, existential and ultimate meanings, and intrinsic qualities, the fact that science is no closer now than it ever was to dealing with them would seem to be clear indication that it is not designed for their investigation.[e] Appeals to the infancy of science only obscure the issue by postponing the question of whether its advances can possibly fill in the lacunae. The answer is no: the change from classical to relativity physics was momentous, but it didn't move physics a whit closer to the untended areas. And we can see why it didn't. For science to enter the domains it has thus far eschewed it would have to relax the demands for objectivity, prediction, control, and number from which its power in quantitative domains derives. We are free, of course, to turn science in this new direction if we want to, but we must realize that every step toward humanizing the enterprise will be a step away from the effectiveness it has thus far manifested. For to repeat, it is precisely from the narrowness of its approach that the power of science derives. An effective and restricted science or one that is ample but does not enable us to control the course of events much more than do art, religion, or psychotherapy—we can define the word as we wish. What is not possible is to have it both ways.

B. Second Demonstration

Whereas the preceding demonstration sought to show how barren a scientific world view would have to be, disclosing perhaps as much of reality as an X-ray negative discloses of a human self, this second demonstration notes that it would also be stunted—or better truncated.

The reasoning behind that statement is as follows.[f]

---

[e] The current (as I write these lines) issue of the *Scientific American* confirms this nonprogress with respect to qualities. Its article by Jerry Fodor on "The Mind-Body Problem" espouses functionalism as the most promising current approach to understanding mental states and operations, but concedes that "the functionalist account does not work for mental states that have qualitative content" (243, no. 7 [January 1981]: 122).

[f] This second demonstration appears three times in these essays, in "Excluded Knowledge," here, and in "Beyond the Modern Western Mind-Set." I have retained it in all three places because, quite apart from the holes that would result if it were removed, the repetitions serve a constructive purpose. The argument they condense is complex, and as it is crucial for perceiving the limitations of our current mind-set, it is important that it sink in. I hope its force will mount each time the argument is encountered.

World views arise from epistemologies which in turn are generated by the motivations that control them. In the seventeenth century Europe hit upon an epistemology (empiricism, the scientific method[g]) that augmented its control dramatically—over nature to start with, but who knew where such control might eventually reach? This increase in power pleased us to the point that we gave this way of knowing right of way. And with that move the die was cast with respect to world view. Empiricism proceeds through sense knowledge, and that which connects with our senses is matter. I do not say that the world view this epistemology has generated is materialism (the view that nothing but matter exists), for our thoughts and feelings are, on the one hand, too conspicuous to be denied and, on the other, too different from what we experience matter to be to be reduced to it. It is safer to dub our world view naturalism, defining this (as I did in section one) as the view (a) that nothing that lacks a material component exists, and (b) that in what does exist the physical component has the final say. That at the level of quantum mechanics this component seems to be "dematerializing" has not shaken our naturalism because matter (however we define it, however ghostly it may seem) remains what we can get our hands on and control. The problem lies deeper than willfulness—wanting to have our way with nature—for even our search for disinterested truth is drawn to naturalism and empiricism. Control includes, importantly, the controlled experiment, and this (more than any other form of validation) inspires confidence.

Now comes the point, the kind of world (view) the will to control can generate. Again let me characterize it negatively. An epistemology that aims relentlessly at control rules out the possibility of transcendence in principle.[h] By transcendence I mean something superior to us by every measure of value we know and some that elude us. To expect a transcendental object to appear on a viewing screen wired by an epistemology that is set for control would be tantamount to expecting color to appear on a television screen that was built for black and white. We can "put nature to the rack," as Bacon advised, because it is our inferior; possessing (in the parts we can get at, at least) neither mind nor freedom, these parts can be

---

[g] I am not overlooking the rational, mathematical component in science, but the crucial role of the controlled experiment gives empiricism the edge.

[h] That modern epistemology so aims was documented in "Excluded Knowledge." I shall not reproduce here the evidence I there assembled; it will be enough to refer the reader to Ernest Gellner's summary verdict on pp. 77–78 above.

pushed around. But if things superior to us exist—extraterrestrial intelligences superior to our own? angels? God?—these are not going to fit into our controlled experiments.[i] It is they who dance circles around us, not we them.

Naturalism's exclusion of things superior to nature combines with its discovery that within nature the superior comes after the inferior, and (to a yet undetermined extent) can be controlled via its inferior components, leaves it no option regarding etiology. Accounting must proceed from inferior to superior, from less to more. Chronologically and developmentally the more comes after the less; causally it comes out of the less, the only other determining principle allowed being chance.[j] In biology (with Darwin) higher forms come after and out of the lower; in sociology (with Marx) the classless society comes after and out of class struggle; in psychology (with Freud) the rational ego comes after and out of the irrational id. Even when the higher has appeared, the thrust is to understand and interpret its workings in terms of the lower. The name for this mode of explanation is, of course, reductionism, and the growth of the scientific world view can be correlated with its advance. For Newton, stars became machines. For Descartes, animals were machines. For Hobbes, society is a machine. For La Mettrie, the human body is a machine. For Pavlov and Skinner, human behavior is mechanical.

C. Third Demonstration

If the preceding demonstration showed that a scientific world view cannot rise above ourselves in the sense of providing a place for anything that is superior to us, this final check on its limitations shows that it cannot even accommodate ourselves. For scientific knowledge is theoretical whereas the bulk of human understanding is practical.[k] Practical understanding cannot be accommodated to theoretical knowledge.

---

[i] Human beings must be kept in the dark if they are to be subjects for controlled experiments in regions where they are free. But transcendental subjects, if they exist, cannot be kept in the dark. By definition they know more than we do.

[j] On reading this, the physicist-theologian William Pollard wrote to me: "But science does not see the significance of chance and therein lies its Achilles Heel." He probes this point powerfully in his *Science and Transcendence*, his contribution to the Eric Rust *Festschrift*, *Creation through Alternative Histories*, and his *Chance and Providence*.

[k] Martin Heidegger appears to have been the first to work out this difference clearly. My account here is indebted to Hubert Dreyfus's treatment of the matter in his "Holism and Hermeneutics," *Review of Metaphysics* 34, no. 1 (September 1980).

Scientific knowledge is theoretical in that it consists of identifiable elements that are systematically related, and this differentiates it sharply from practical knowing—knowing how to ride a bicycle, say, or how to swim. In these latter cases our knowledge proceeds in almost total oblivion of the components involved—muscles, nerves, cells, and the like—and their coordinations. It is a "knowing how," rather than a "knowing that."

Another way to put the difference is to say that theoretical knowledge is context-free whereas practical understanding is not. Once we consciously identify something our minds can isolate it from its context. In looking at a vase I cannot separate my sensation of blue from the vase, but once my mind tells me that the vase *is* blue, though the copula purports to join blueness to vase, in a far more fateful way it disjoins the two. For I can now think blueness without vase and this frees me to move it around my conceptual world at will. In abstracting—extracting—blueness from vase, cognition makes it context free.

Science capitalizes on this freedom from context and tries to show us a contextless world, a view of things that is not affected by even the fact that it derives from our human angle of vision. And when it goes on to try to understand human beings (through the social sciences), this goal continues. It searches for behavior ingredients that are invariant—the same regardless of their context—and the lawful relations these exhibit. The theories that summarize these relations currently take the form of formal models in which the facts are context-free elements or attributes or features or information bits, and the model is a computer program or flow chart showing how such elements are combined to produce complex individual or social behavior.

That these models, be they in structural anthropology, cognitive psychology, or decision analysis, have succeeded no better than their predecessors in enabling their practitioners to predict, or in snowballing into a unified theory of man that compares in any way to the unified view of nature that undergirds the physical sciences, should not surprise us, for to return to the nub of this third demonstration, most human knowledge is not theoretical but practical, and even theoretical knowledge rides on a practical base. Practical knowing can no more be separated from its context (to become available to abstract theory) than knowing how to swim can be separated from water. Through cultivated body responses, the "tentacles" of our swimming skill grip the physical world like a root system; and in social skills it is the same, the difference being only that here the context is a background of shared beliefs and practices which we internalize through imitation. Social skills, such as how far to stand from a conversational partner depending on age, sex, status, and purpose embody a whole cultural interpretation of what it means to be a human being, what a material object is, and (more generally) what counts as real. Heidegger, Merleau-Ponty, and Wittgenstein have shown convincingly, I believe, that this inherited background of practices can never be spelled out in a theory (to be fed into a computer), first, because it is so pervasive that we cannot stand outside it to make it an object of analysis, but even more because in the last resort it is not composed of cognitive features such as beliefs and assumptions at all, but rather of habits and customs, the sort of subtle skills which we exhibit in our everyday interaction with things and people—what Michel Foucault calls micropractices. No one has the slightest idea how to construct formal rules for the skills involved in swimming or speaking a language, let alone those embodying our understanding of what it means to be a human being and live a human life.

III. THEOLOGICAL COMPROMISE?

That was a long section, so let me reiterate its point. Believing that the decline in our sense of transcendence is a loss, and that the chief reason for the decline has been the rise of a rival outlook presumed to be scientific, I think that it is important to show that that supposition is mistaken. Lacking space to show point by point where the error enters, I am going (in this statement) after the notion of a scientific world view itself, presenting three lines of argument that converge in the conclusion that there can be no such thing. When we find someone writing that "science is the measure of all things, of what is that it is, and of what is not that it is not,"[3] we know automatically that scientism, not science, is speaking.

But now comes the touchy part. Of the five postures Richard Niebuhr showed the church to have assumed toward culture in the course of its history—against it, with it, above it, paradoxical toward it, and with design to transform it[4]—we are clearly in a "with culture" phase; Vatican II formalized this for Roman Catholicism and Bultmann's victory over Barth is a weather vane for Protestantism. But if our culture is riddled with scientism—the problem being, as Victor Frankl puts it, not that the scientists are specializing, but that the specialists are generalizing—in being *with* culture, the church runs the danger of scientistic rub off.

There is no way to insure against this danger, but the guidelines (at least) seem clear. It goes without saying that theologians should respect the proven findings of science, and can continue to affirm as they have (in the past two decades especially) that:

> Scientists are no less blessed with *human virtues* than the rest of us. Their work does not pull against their idealism, good will, and natural piety (Harold Schilling, William Pollard, Ian Barbour).
>
> Their *intellectual virtues* are not mechanical—limited to logic and linear thinking. Great science requires as much imagination, inspiration, and "art" as any other creative endeavor (Abraham Maslow, Michael Polanyi).
>
> Equally, as institution, science is as *fallible* as other social efforts. False starts, blind alleys, in-house vendettas and outright mistakes plague it as much as they do the church (Thomas Kuhn, James Watson's *The Double Helix,* and again Polanyi).

These commonalities, though, should not be allowed to obscure the distinctiveness of scientific knowing, and the limited character of the conclusions that can issue from that distinctiveness.

The first of these two dividing, rather than reconciling, tasks is currently complicated by a move within the philosophy of science itself that slurs the difference between scientific and other ways of knowing. Because at advanced levels the components of science are not tested against experience one by one but only as a whole via theories, it is now generally accepted that scientific facts are theory laden. In verifying a theory we move in a circle from hypothesis to data, data to hypothesis, without ever encountering any bare facts which could call the whole theory into question. From this (now recognized) holistic character of science—the point, to repeat, that its facts, like most others, have to be "interpreted" in the light of the systems in which they appear[5]—this new thrust concludes that science doesn't differ in kind from other self-contained systems of thought such as common sense, or even witchcraft. Paul Feyerabend's *Against Method* pushes this claim to anarchist extremes, but its basic point, which can be traced back to Pierre Duhem in the last century, appears in varying degrees in the writings of N. R. Hanson, Willard Quine, and Richard Rorty.

We can agree that science is holistic, but the theoretical character of its holism, which gestalts explicitly identified, context-free components, still differentiates it from other kinds of holism; this was the burden of the third demonstration in the preceding section. The difference must be kept in mind. For if we lose sight of the distinctive, restricted way science goes about knowledge we will think that its findings harbor more implications for theology than they logically can.

As these implications slope toward naturalism, evolution,[1] and progress, if we insist on drawing them—or, what is more common, if we lower our guard, in which case they are sure to enter undetected—theology will suffer. I think I see this happening. I say this tentatively. Kennett Roshi of Mount Shasta Zen Abbey once remarked that she was working on a new *ko'an*, "I could be wrong," and I would like to have that apply to the balance of this section.

So numerous are the theological innovations of modernity that one wonders if, at some unconscious level, they may not be fed by the assumption that as scientific knowledge is cumulative, all knowledge should be.[m] Be that as it may, when I scan the content of these innovations, what I mostly see is loss—loss that has been suffered, not from the proven facts of science, but from vapors that

---

[1] I use this word to refer, not to the proven facts of biology and the fossil record, but to the theory (assumed to be established by those facts) which claims that natural selection working on chance mutations adequately accounts for how we got here. No major theologian I know is currently challenging this doctrine—"the most influential teaching of the modern age," as E. F. Schumacher calls it—leaving it to Billy Graham and fundamentalist creationists on the one hand, and concerned laymen like Schumacher himself and secularists like Arthur Koestler on the other, to expose this "crumbling citadel," as Koestler calls it. See Arthur Koestler, *Janus: A Summing Up* (New York: Vintage Books, 1979), pp. 165–92; E. F. Schumacher, *A Guide for the Perplexed* (New York: Harper and Row, 1977), pp. 111–16; and my own *Forgotten Truth*, pp. 126–42. The point is crucial, and in the present book I return to it on pp. 169–74.

[m] For my part, I find it more likely that our forefathers—less harried by life's accelerated pace, less deluged and distracted by avalanches of information, less insulated from illness, death, and nature generally—had the theological edge. I find what Origen said of St. Paul, that he understood Moses far better than we can, altogether plausible.

rise from them like steam, obscuring our sight. (1) Personalism concludes that we must relieve God of either his omnipotence or his goodness. (2) Bultmann's demythologizing rides the dismantling of a pre-Copernican picture of the physical universe to dismantle, in fact, the great chain of being. If only because of what Heidegger (from whom Bultmann draws) will not permit us to *say,* on pain of inauthentic objectivizing, I do not see his Being as a match for either the living God of the Bible or the *ens perfectissimum* of medieval theology. (3) The theology of hope historicizes Christian expectations and introduces development into God, who in ways is "not yet." (4) Teilhard de Chardin's notion of Christ as "the term of evolution," upsets his alpha-omega balance and makes meaning turn on the fate of nature.

(5) As I was myself weaned on process theology, I shall give it three paragraphs, beginning again with loss. It deprives God of ultimacy, reserving that for three inexplicable givens: creativity, eternal objects, and the structure of actual occasions.[n] It rules out the possibility of a concrete, timeless perfection; only abstract entities (eternal objects) are eternal. And its replaces subjective human immortality with an objective version in which we are remembered by God; the traditional teaching that we must all one day awaken from life's dream into other dimensions in which the lie shrivels, the fiction is destroyed, and all deceptions are swept away, is done away with. On what authority, save the naturalism to which process theology is beholden? We can at least be clear, this essay has argued, that science doesn't force that naturalism on us.

Process theologians themselves, of course, do not see these revisions as losses, for to them classical theism is incoherent. Had their notion of coherence ruled at Nicea and Chalcedon, the creeds could not have come down to us as they have. Or to approach the point from a contemporary angle, is there any "incoherence" in classical theism—many are charged—that does not have its analogy in the paradoxes of quantum mechanics, and cannot, with deep discernment, be brought under Niels Bohr's claim that, whereas the oppo-

---

[n] "The direction is to accept without hesitation or embarrassment the distinction between ultimate reality and God, and to recognize that the God of the Bible . . . is a manifestation of ultimate reality—not the name of that reality" (John Cobb, "Can a Christian Be a Buddhist, Too?," *Japanese Religions,* December 1978, p. 11).

site of a small truth is false, the opposite of a great truth is another great truth?

I was not myself conscious of the loss in this "updated"⁰ Christianity until, seeking to expand my horizons through the study of world religions, I came (first) on the Vedanta, whereupon I found that my interest in process theology dropped markedly, and with it my interest in Christianity until I discovered that its classical expressions include everything of importance I had discovered in the Upanishads. Why, then, is this loss—process theology—being inflicted on Christians? (That is a strong charge. I keep repeating to myself, like the Jesus Prayer, "I could be wrong, I could be wrong!") Because—I answer from introspection, it being a part of my former self that I am trying to understand—theologians saw in Whitehead the prospect of reconciling religion with modern science. This is a chancy move. As Jeremy Bernstein observed in his review of Fritjof Capra's *The Tao of Physics,* "to hitch a religious philosophy to a contemporary science is a sure route to its obsolescence, [for] the science of the present will look as antiquated to our successors as much of nineteenth-century science looks to us now."[6] Whitehead's philosophy of organism, focusing in its doctrine of prehensions, was modeled on (and thereby powered by) the most sophisticated science of its day; it followed carefully Einstein's prescription, required by his relativity theory, that as no coherent concept of an independently existent particle is possible, reality should be regarded as constituted of fields whose localized pulses do not end abruptly but spread to arbitrarily large distances with decreasing force. As this banished the spectre of clockwork mechanism, which for three hundred years had haunted theology with its view of the world as constituted of entities which are outside of each other in the sense that they exist independently in different regions of space (and time) and interact through forces that do not bring about any changes in their essential natures, it was a thrilling synthesis—I speak for myself; I felt it. But science keeps moving, and it now appears that the unified field theory Einstein had hoped for is not going to happen short of another paradigm change, which would carry us beyond

---

⁰ Schubert Ogden claims that process theology has achieved "something like a Heideggerian 'dismantling' (*Destruktion*) of the history of philosophical theology" (*The Reality of God* [New York: Harper and Row, 1977], p. 48).

Einstein and Bohr, and therefore beyond Whitehead. Relativity and quantum theory proceed from such opposite premises that it seems impossible for either to accommodate the other.[p] "What is probably needed," David Bohm writes,

> is a qualitatively new theory, from which both relativity and quantum theory are to be derived as abstractions. . . . The best place to begin is with what they have basically in common. This is undivided wholeness. Though each comes to such wholeness in a different way, it is clear that it is this to which they are both fundamentally pointing.[7]

Undivided wholeness sounds more like God's simplicity (in its technical medieval sense) than like the time-involved creativity and discrete eternal objects Whitehead took for ultimates.

IV. SCIENCE AS SYMBOL

It is possible that the preceding section was squandered in what Freud called "the narcissism of small differences," though I do not think so. In any case, though I have exhausted the space allotted me, I do not want to end without noting that there is another side to the science/theology question, one that is very different and filled with possibilities that counter the pitfalls I have dwelt on here. If, instead of rummaging through science for direct, literal clues to the nature of reality, we could outgrow this fundamentalism and read science allegorically, we would find sermons in cloud chambers. That the deeper science advances into nature the more integrated it finds it, lends resonance to (though it does not prove) the faith claim that the same holds for being as a whole: God, who is all in all, is likewise one. Or again, that science has found reality in its physical aspect to be incomparably more majestic and awesome than we had supposed suggests—it does not prove—that if we could see the full picture we would find its qualitative depths to be as much beyond what we normally suppose as science has shown its quantitative ones to be.[q]

And remember, we are speaking of light-years.

---

[p] Relativity theory requires continuity, strict causality, and locality. Quantum theory requires noncontinuity, noncausality, and nonlocality.

[q] Chapter five of my *Forgotten Truth* is devoted to the symbolic power latent in science today.

NOTES

1. *Works,* ed. J. Spedding and R. L. Ellis (London, 1858), 4:365.
2. Jacques Monod, *Chance and Necessity* (New York: Random House, 1972), p. 21.
3. Wilfred Sellars, *Science, Perception, and Reality* (New York: Humanities Press, 1963), p. 173.
4. *Christ and Culture* (New York: Harper and Brothers, 1956).
5. It is interesting to find the word *hermeneutics,* and names like Heidegger and Hans-Georg Gadamer, now surfacing in the philosophy of science.
6. *American Scholar* 48 (Winter 1978–1979): 8.
7. *Wholeness and the Implicate Order* (London: Routledge & Kegan Paul, 1980), p. 176.

·7·

A FOOTNOTE ON
TEILHARD DE CHARDIN*

If I were to rewrite *Forgotten Truth,* I would omit the passage in which I quote, without sufficient explanation, a scathing paragraph from P. B. Medawar's review of Teilhard de Chardin's *The Phenomenon of Man.* My intent was to counter what looked like a headlong rush of theology into the arms of science, the dangers of which were the burden of the preceding essay, but my summary treatment of Teilhard was certainly not fair to him. So when Thomas King, S.J., invited me to respond to a paper that formed a part of the symposium on "Teilhard and the Unity of Knowledge" that was held at Georgetown University in May, 1981, I used the occasion to explain, and to some degree apologize for, the injustice.

As the final respondent in this symposium I propose to turn our thoughts back to Teilhard's, and I shall initiate that move with a confession. We know that an honest confession is good for the soul. Unfortunately it tends to be bad for the reputation, but I shall make mine anyway. I may be the only one on the panel of this symposium who has gone to print in criticism of Teilhard. Not in my own words, to be sure, but in *Forgotten Truth* I quote Medawar's review of *The Phenomenon of Man* which (as many of you know) was harsh. Perhaps it was for that quotation that I was invited to this conference—for my education, surely; possibly for conversion; and (as I glance nervously around this auditorium) conceivably for ambush. In any case, something constructive has hap-

* Reprinted with permission and negligible changes from Thomas King, ed., *Teilhard and the Unity of Knowledge* (Washington, D.C.: Georgetown University Press, 1982).

pened. I shall not pretend that all my difficulties with Teilhard's vision have been resolved, but this symposium has given me a new and constructive way to look at his enterprise, and this is helpful. I shall say what that new way is, but first my difficulties.

1. The first of these concerns a claim found at the beginning of *The Phenomenon of Man* where Teilhard says that the book should not be read as a metaphysical or theological work; it should be read purely and simply as a scientific treatise. Fifteen years of teaching at M.I.T. has made me sensitive to the way that word "science" is used. I realize that in Europe the word has a broader connotation, *Wissenschaft,* but in the English-speaking world science has come to refer to the natural sciences; if we speak of social science, the word "social" functions as a diminutive to distinguish it from science proper. When not qualified, science in our society connotes things like the space shuttle and open-heart surgery—discoveries about nature that can be experimentally confirmed and produce technological spin-off. No one, I suppose, sees Teilhard's theses as possessing these particular virtues, so it seems to me to confuse issues to call them scientific. Compatible with science, surely; but to suggest that they are themselves scientific theses is to stretch things. The National Endowment for the Humanities saw fit to support this symposium. I doubt that the National Science Foundation would have deemed it within its jurisdiction.

2. This may be semantic lintpicking, but beyond it looms Teilhard's whole effort to ground theology *in* science. My concern here stems from the fact that science changes—several of our previous speakers have alluded to this point. Jeremy Bernstein, the Princeton physicist who writes for *The American Scholar,* put the matter well in a column on Fritjof Capra's *The Tao of Physics* a year or two back. He said that if he were an Indian guru and a physicist approached him proposing that they work out a joint proclamation on the nature of reality, he would flee to the Himalayas in escape. For "to hitch a religious philosophy to contemporary science is a sure route to its obsolescence. The science of the present will look as antiquated to our successors as nineteenth-century science looks to us now." I speak with some feeling on this point having had my own fingers burned. I cut my theological teeth on Whitehead's process philosophy, but came in time to abandon it out of conviction that Whitehead had forged his cosmology to accommodate Einstein, and

great as Einstein was, he is not forever. Einstein had hoped for a unified field theory that would integrate relativity theory and quantum mechanics, and we now see that that is not going to happen. We need a framework beyond both Einstein and Whitehead, one which (for our latter twentieth century) David Bohm seems to be exploring imaginatively. The "undifferentiated wholeness" of Bohm's implicate order seems closer to the divine simplicity of the Middle Ages than to the ontology of Whitehead.

3. Not only does science change; if we try to accommodate our ontology to it, it constricts. Science is a technique for dealing with one region of reality, the material world. But that's not the whole of reality; indeed, it is its lowest level. When to (a) the fact that the crux of science is the controlled experiment, we add (b) the further fact that we can control only what is inferior to us, we see that if there is anything that in every respect including intelligence is superior to us—angels? God?—these are not going to "show" in a scientific world view. If such superiors exist they are not going to fit into controlled experiments for the sufficient reason that it is they who dance circles around us, not we them. If only things that are inferior to us can appear in a scientific view finder, to tie theology too closely to science will be to short-circuit it.

4. I have problems, too, with the evolution that figures so prominently in Teilhard's scheme because the notion is fiercely ambiguous. On the one hand, it refers to the fossil record, the evidence that higher forms of life came *after* simpler forms; no one has trouble with that—even Genesis says as much. But evolution also refers to a theory which claims not just that higher forms came after simpler forms but *out* of them. With no purpose anywhere admixed, we must add, if the theory is to be scientific, for the canons of science are violated the moment purpose is introduced. In Jacques Monod's formulation of the point, "the cornerstone of scientific method . . . is the *systematic* denial that 'true' knowledge can be got at by interpreting phenomena in terms of final causes—that is to say, of 'purpose.'" But God is a final cause, so I get nervous when I see theologians rushing into the arms of evolution as a scientific theory. This is quite apart from the difficulties the theory currently faces within science itself. Professor Weiner wisely cautioned us to be careful about that theory; it is in more trouble than most laypersons realize. Arthur Koestler calls it "a citadel in ruins."

5. My last problem concerns time. Time is so central to Teilhard's vision that it reads as if it were an ultimate. Yet even scientists—David Bohm again, and John Wheeler—are now saying that time seems to be relative rather than absolute, provisional rather than final. I fidget when I find theologians according to process a status larger than even scientists will admit.

Now let me briefly register the change that has occurred in my attitude toward Teilhard's work that this symposium has effected. It began last weekend when at another conference I was having breakfast with Ewert Cousins, whose name many of you will recognize. I knew that he had been active in the Teilhard Society, so I said, "Help me. I am going to a Teilhard symposium next week and though I look forward to it, I am nervous. Let me tell you what I see; then you tell me what I should hear." So I listed for him my five problems, much as I have told them to you. And Ewert did indeed tell me what I should hear, as follows:

"Just as Dante used the Ptolemaic cosmology of his day as symbolic framework for *The Divine Comedy,* so Teilhard uses the cosmology of our time to frame his vision. In both cases the vision exceeds the cosmology, and is not endangered should the cosmology be superceded."

I could hear that, and it helped me as I turned back to Teilhard anticipating this conference. If we do not read him like fundamentalists, as if he were writing literal science, but instead read his "science" allegorically and symbolically, we can see how his writings have healing power. This conference testifies to that power; I, like you, know many who have been healed by his vision—Lillian Smith was one. So I use this occasion to voice my regrets that in alluding to Teilhard in the past I was so occupied with the problems he posed for me that I had not then the wit to see how his vision can be read constructively.

Part Four

THE WAY OUT

Sensibilities differ, and mine (clearly) are better tuned to the past than to the future. I see the optimism of our New Age Aquarians cancelled by the pessimism of our doomsday Cassandras and find myself hamstrung between them. If I could have my way I would redirect, unopened to its opposite numbers, the mail that reaches me from both camps. Let them fight it out while I hold their coats, for I cannot detect a futuristic gene in my makeup.

Obviously, then, the word "beyond" in this book's title does not portend prediction. This final section will not crystal-ball the future, trying to foresee what the ethos of the twenty-first century will look like. As for what it should look like, this has already been proposed; our hope lies in returning to an outlook which in its broad outlines is carried in the bloodstream of the human race.

The first essay in this closing section begins by reviewing the strictures the modern Western mind-set imposes against such a return, stricture being defined (as in the *Oxford English Dictionary*) as "a morbid contraction of some canal or duct in the body"—and goes on from there to suggest in contemporary idiom what an outlook released from those strictures might look like. This is followed by a statement titled "Checkpoints" which directs attention to some fine lines on the mind-set in question that suggest developing fissures; these should be watched carefully to see if they widen into cracks through which the needed breakthrough can be effected. "The Sacred Unconscious" asks how the human self might appear if seen in its full stature, while "The Incredible Assumption" capsules the thesis of the book as a whole and rounds it off in a kind of flourish.

·8·

BEYOND THE MODERN
WESTERN MIND-SET*

I n "Excluded Knowledge," an essay that appeared in an earlier
issue of this journal,[1] I argued that world views arise from epistemologies, which in turn are generated by the motivations that
control them. In the seventeenth century Europe hit on an epistemology (empiricism, the scientific method[2]) that augmented its
control dramatically—over nature to start with. But who knew
where such control might eventually reach? This increase in our
power pleased us to the point that we gave this way of knowing right
of way. And with that move the die was cast with respect to world
view. Empiricism proceeds through sense knowledge, and that
which connects with our senses is matter. I do not say that the world
view this epistemology has generated is materialism (the view that
nothing but matter exists), for our thoughts and feelings are, on the
one hand, too conspicuous to be denied and, on the other, too
different from what we experience matter to be, to be reduced to it.
It is safer to dub our modern Western world view naturalism, this
being defined as the view that (a) nothing that lacks a material
component exists, and (b) in what does exist the physical component has the final say.

It is ironic that the science that lured us into this world view now
seems to be abandoning it. With each successive probe, matter had
been growing more ethereal even before Einstein discovered that
mass and energy are convertible. What this energy is no one quite
knows. If a thimbleful of vacuum contains more energy than all the

---

* Reprinted with permission from *Teachers College Record* 82, no. 3 (Spring 1981).

atomic energy in the universe,[a] it cannot be less powerful than when it is impounded in mass; but as the reference to vacuum emphasizes, in its free state it seems less substantial. Priestly and Boscovitch argued early on that Newton's acceptance of the Greek view that atoms are impenetrable was simple-minded; they are better conceived as mathematical points surrounded by fields of forces that repel up to a point, then attract with the inverse square of the distance. Now that we have split atoms we know that Priestly and Boscovitch were wrong; atoms do have size. But their point may still hold for electrons. Some current experiments suggest that they have a finite size, others that they do not. If something has no size, or no definite position as in the case of particles before they are subject to position measurements, are they still matter? The message that reaches us from frontier physics seems to be that the further we track matter toward its causal origins, the more it sheds the attributes it wears in the "middle region" of size that our senses register, until at some vanishing point on the horizon it seems to drop these attributes altogether to becoming something we can scarcely guess—disappearing, perhaps, into David Bohm's implicate order.[b]

This ghostly writing has been on the wall for the better part of our century, but it has not shaken our naturalism, which bids to exit this century more entrenched, if anything, than when it entered it. This is because matter remains what we can get at and control. The problem lies deeper than willfulness—wanting to have our way over nature—for even our search for disinterested truth is drawn to naturalism and empiricism. Control includes, importantly, the controlled experiment, and this, more than any other form of validation, inspires confidence. Bertrand Russell's mid-century BBC pronouncement that "what science cannot tell us, mankind cannot know" is absurd as it stands, but if we amend it to read" cannot collectively know for sure," it becomes less so. Propositionalized, this introductory point can be indicated as follows:

---

[a] See John Wheeler's address to the American Physical Society in January 1967 as summarized in Walter Sullivan, "Smallest of the Small," *New York Times,* 5 February 1967. The basic principle involved is that "the amount of energy associated with light corpuscles increases as the size is reduced. . . . The energy necessary to create a proton is contained in a light pulse only about 10^{-13} centimeters in diameter. And the energy of a million protons would be contained in a light pulse a million times smaller (Arthur Young, *Which Way Out?* [Berkeley: Robert Briggs Associates, 1980], p. 2).

[b] David Bohm, *Wholeness and the Implicate Order* (London: Routledge & Kegan Paul, 1980). Professor Bohm was in the audience when the initial draft of this paper was presented. When I came to this line I was gratified to see him nod in agreement.

Matter is that which (with whatever required amplification) registers on our senses.

Our senses are where our worlds overlap.

The parts of our worlds that overlap are the parts we trust most, for we are social creatures: down isolation's path lies madness.

It is all so plausible. To restate the point only slightly:

Seeing is believing, touching is truth (an old American proverb).

Science's extension of our seeing and touching has augmented our power and enabled us to solve certain problems spectacularly.

With the collectivizing of society we look increasingly to government to solve our problems, while the government relies on science to help it do so.

Everywhere accent falls on the sense domain. It would be surprising if naturalism were not our world view and empiricism our favored noetic probe.

But problems abound. "Our society is not working well and all signs indicate it will work less well in the future," sociologist Robert Bellah told the Woodstock symposium on which this issue of the *Record* is based. We need to look at these problems, but first I should describe more systematically the outlook that contributes to them.

I. WHAT THE MODERN WESTERN MIND-SET IS

I think I see more clearly now than when I wrote either "Excluded Knowledge" or the book out of which that essay derived, *Forgotten Truth*, what the Modern Western Mind-set (hereafter MWM) is. The clue to it can be stated in a single sentence: *An epistemology that aims relentlessly at control rules out the possibility of transcendence in principle.*[c] By transcendence I mean something that is better than we are by every measure of value we know and some that elude us. To expect a transcendental object to appear on a viewing screen wired by an epistemology that aims at control would

---

[c] That current epistemology *is* geared to control has been argued in earlier essays, so I shall not remarshall the evidence here. See especially pp. 77–78 above.

be tantamount to expecting the melody as well as the lyrics of a song to issue from a printout typewriter. We can "put nature to the rack," as Bacon advised, because it is inferior to us; possessing (in its elemental parts at least) neither mind nor freedom in the genuine sense, these parts can be pushed around. But if things that are superior to us exist, they are not going to fit into our controlled experiments, any more than self-consciousness or advanced forms of abstract thinking would fit into (and hence be brought to light by) experiments woodchucks hypothetically might devise. It being as impossible for us to acquire "effective knowledge" (see p. 77 above) over them as it is to nail a drop of mercury with our thumb, an epistemology that drives single-mindedly toward effective knowledge is not going to allow transcendent realities to exist.[d]

It follows that accounting can proceed only from the bottom up—from inferior to superior, from less to more. Chronologically and developmentally the more comes after the less; causally it comes out of the less, the only other determining principle allowed being chance, which of course is a nonprinciple, the absence of a principle. Even when the higher has appeared, the thrust is to understand and interpret its workings in terms of the lower. The name for this mode of explanation is, of course, reductionism,[e] and the growth of the MWM can be correlated with its advance. For Newton, stars became machines. For Descartes animals were machines. For Hobbes society is a machine. For La Mettrie the human body is a machine. For Pavlov and Skinner, human behavior is mechanical.

> *How many boxes,*
> *How many stars;*
> *How long, O Lord,*
> *Till they open the bars.*[3]

This reductionistic momentum has not abated. Beginning with consciousness, we find Daniel Dennett telling us that "materialism in one form or another is the reigning orthodoxy among philoso-

---

[d] Signs of this are everywhere, but I shall confine myself to a single example, drawn from a participant at the Woodstock symposium. Owen Barfield points out that "the eighteenth century essay was allowed . . . to 'bring in' religion [i.e., transcendence], which is exactly what the twentieth century was not allowed to do. Not on any account" (*Journal of the American Academy of Religion* 47/2, Supplement (June 1979): 221–22).

[e] The belief that human activities can be "reduced" to—for example, explained by—the behavior of lower animals and that these in turn can be reduced to the physical laws that govern inanimate matter. For a full-scale critique of this belief see Arthur Koestler and James Smythies, *Beyond Reductionism* (New York: Macmillan, 1970).

phers of mind"[4] and Carl Sagan saying in his best-selling *The Dragons of Eden* that his "fundamental premise about the brain is that its workings—what we sometimes call 'mind'—are a consequence of its anatomy and physiology and nothing more."[5] On our way from psychology to biology we cross sociology, where attempts to explain human behavior in terms of continuities with lower forms of life have spawned a vigorous subdiscipline, sociobiology. As this is currently one of the liveliest crossdisciplinary subjects on university campuses, I shall reserve it for separate treatment and pass on to biology. "Biologists," Harold Morowitz, professor of molecular biophysics and biochemistry at Yale tells us, "have been moving relentlessly toward . . . hard-core materialism."[6] Francis Crick, codiscoverer of DNA, agrees: "The ultimate aim of the modern movement in biology is to explain all biology in terms of physics and chemistry."[7] Going back to Morowitz: As "physiologists study the activity of living cells in terms of processes carried out by organelles and other subcellular entities, the study of life at all levels, from social to molecular behavior, has in modern times relied on reductionism as the chief explanatory concept."[8] In nonlife, too, we may add; in geology, for example, the formations and properties of minerals are described using the features of the constituent crystals. To close the loop by returning to the top of the ladder, we find that not just mind in general but its finest achievements are approached from below. Ethnocriticism has emerged as the attempt to understand works of art in terms of animal behavior. A sample on my desk proposes to shed light on three literary classics—Moliere's *The Would-be Gentleman,* Diderot's *Rameau's Nephew,* and Zola's *Germinal*—by showing that "play" serves the same function in these works as it does in the animal kingdom. "Culture has to do the same job that instinct had been doing."[9]

This spot-check shows how widely the reductionistic approach is invoked. But I promised to say something about sociobiology. So let me conclude this section on what the MWM is with a quick look at the way reductionism proceeds in its province.

The Naked Ape and *The Territorial Imperative* are discounted for the glib way they transposed raw, isolated data from one species to another, but their search for biological roots of human behavior continues to be pushed to the hilt. Whether through Pavlov's dogs, Skinner's pigeons and rats, or Lorenz's greylag geese, the hope everywhere is to discover continuities, for only in lower registers are explanations for our basic propensities available. Piaget details continuities in play[10] and speech, seeing the latter as deriving from structures of thought that have their roots in sensorimotor mechanisms that are deeper than linguistics.[11] John Bowlby's fifteen-year, three-volume study *Attachment and Loss* is a detailed effort to bridge the gap between innate patterns of attachment in mammals and the attachment/loss complex in the human baby. Let me be clear: insofar as such studies simply indicate traits we share with other life forms, they do no harm and indeed some good, for until recently the modern world has made too much of the human/subhuman divide. And there are practical lessons to be learned from the similarities. Bowlby's findings on the crucial role of early emotional attachments in the development of life forms generally, for example, might induce us to pay more attention to this area as we relate to our own children. If his study had concluded simply that "the basic structure of man's behavioral equipment resembles that of infrahuman species," there could be no objection. What must be watched is the sentence that follows, where he moves from the observation that "the early form is not superseded" to the inference that "it [the infrahuman form] shall *determine* the overall pattern."[12] Here the inferior-causes-superior assumption appears in full display.

It is Harvard's Edward O. Wilson, though, who has moved sociobiology onto the pages of *The New York Review of Books* and made it a lively public topic, so his views deserve a paragraph or two in their own right. Like other sociobiologists, he draws on data from life forms generally to reason that human behavior, including actions and choices traditionally explained in terms of idealism and disinterested love of others, is ultimately to be understood as genetically determined. Even when we behave "nobly" we are in fact responding to genetic conditioning that moves to seek our own interests or those of our kinship group.[13]

Wilson divides altruism into two kinds. Soft-core altruism looks like it is directed toward the welfare of others but actually redounds circuitously to its agent's benefit. Hardcore altruism is likewise disguised self-interest, but here the interested agent is not the individual organism, who may even sacrifice his life; it is the species whose will prevails. From the species' point of view individuals exist merely to produce genes and serve as their temporary carriers: "The organism is only DNA's way of making more DNA."[14] As mutual aid between its members helps a species to survive, genes that induce the hypothalamus and limbic systems of the brain to entertain warm feelings for one's fellows have a "Darwinian edge" and turn out to be winners. This is why we lay down our lives for our friends;[f] our genes prompt us to do so.

While the West's "brain," which for present purposes we can equate with the modern university, rolls ever further down the reductionistic path, other centers of society—our emotions, for example, as they find expression through our artists, and our wills, as evidenced in part by rise in crime and senseless vandalism—protest. These other centers of our selves feel that they are being dragged, kicking and screaming, down an ever-darkening tunnel. We need to listen to their protests, for they force us to ask if it is possible to move toward a world view that, without compromising reason or evidence in the slightest, would allow more room to the sides of our selves that our current world view constricts.

II. THE NEED FOR A DIFFERENT OUTLOOK

When individuals suffer the loss of something that implicates their sense of self—a spouse, a child, whatever it is that gives their life its focus and meaning—they grow ill; not invariably, but in greater proportion. They become more prone to cancer, for one thing. Here is a clear and direct causal flow from mind to matter. In dynamics it parallels exactly the way hypnosis can remove warts, and placebos cause the brain to secrete more pain-relieving endorphins. In all these cases a mental change effects a bodily one. But the MWM does

---

[f] These friends cannot be four-footed, feathered, or furry though—much less leafy and flowery. To be kind to the point of sacrificing human interests for these—restraining our predatory impulses towards the whales, say—is irrational, for in genetic ethics (the opening section of *Sociobiology* is titled "The Morality of the Gene") "rational" is what favors species survival.

It is irrational to defer to other species unless there is a gene that has caught on to the fact that species need environments to sustain them—I enter this suggestion on my own to caricature the lengths to which sociobiology has already stretched evidence in the interests of theory (see Marvin Harris, *Cultural Materialism;* Richard Dawkins, *The Selfish Gene;* and Stuart Hampshire, "The Illusion of Sociobiology," *The New York Review of Books,* 12 October 1978). Wilson is now quoted as saying that by "gene" he does not mean the actual physical entities we can see with electron microscopes. Officially he claims only that biological findings might plausibly be used to explain human behavior. But his suggestion meshes so neatly with current styles of explanation that a dropped hint is enough to place its author in vast demand. Sociologists and psychologists are already working with sociobiological hypotheses as if they were tested theories—Pierre van den Berghe and David Barash are examples.

not know what to do with mind; Barbara Brown tells of a symposium in which a scientist reacted to the suggestion that the mind is emerging as a new tool for medicine by roaring to the audience, "Talking about mind will set medicine back fifty years!"[15] We understand something of how the brain works, and, yes, through depth psychology something of how the mind works too. But when it comes to infusing the mind with motivation and meaning, the MWM is helpless.

In itself this can be excused, since anyone who claimed to have techniques for such infusion would be a charlatan. What is not attractive is the way the MWM works to erode the meaning lives already have. D. and C. Johnson report a pattern of disorder among Sioux Indians called *tawatl ye sni,* "totally discouraged." The syndrome involves feelings of helplessness and thoughts of death: "There is no way out . . . there's nothing he can do."[16] Conditions on the Dakota reservations doubtless go a long way toward accounting for this syndrome, but it would be naive to think that the near collapse of the Native American world view is not also a factor. The six-volume *Handbook of Cross-Cultural Psychology,* which includes the Johnsons' study, illustrates how the MWM facilitates this collapse.[g] If the Sioux feels himself to be in touch with higher forces, this is because his "reality bounds are not as firmly established as is the case in certain Western societies."[17] If he senses his life to be in the hands of a higher power—well, this "actually serves a useful function in alleviating the stress of life."[18] The clinical, patronizing term for this function is, of course, compensation.

The maladies in our personal lives have become psychological and so have moved into an area we have abandoned. That psychology courses remain the most popular college electives and *Psychology Today* is a booming success does not counter this observation. As the passage on reductionism in the preceding section indicates, we have abandoned the mind by converting to efforts to understand it in terms of things other than itself and lower than itself.

The consequences of this abandonment for our civilization as a whole are difficult to assess. Who is to tell us? Let me opt this time

[g] Or the collapse of any world view with a religious component, for that matter. Edward Wilson says sociobiology is forced to conclude that "the predisposition to religious belief is the most complex and powerful force in the human mind"; but whereas elsewhere complexity is a biological virtue, here it shows only that the religious impulse is "in all probability ineradicable" (Edward O. Wilson, *On Human Nature* [New York: Bantam Books, 1978], p. 176).

around for Alexander Solzhenitsyn, focusing on his 1978 commencement address at Harvard University.[19] As an exile, he is not likely to downgrade us in favor of Soviet Russia; he sees socialism of any type and shade as leading to a total destruction of the human spirit and to a leveling of mankind into death. But as an outside observer he may be able to see us more objectively than we see ourselves. And what he sees in the West today is "spiritual exhaustion."[20]

> How short a time ago . . . the small world of modern Europe was easily seizing colonies all over the globe. . . . It all seemed an overwhelming success. . . . Western society expanded in a triumph of human independence and power. And all of a sudden the twentieth century brought the clear realization of this society's fragility.[21]

If Solzhenitsyn saw only political factors as responsible for this twentieth-century reversal I would not be quoting him here. As it is, his diagnosis points directly to the concern of this essay.

> How did the West decline from its triumphal march to its present debility? Have there been fatal turns and losses of direction in its development? It does not seem so. The West kept advancing steadily in accordance with its proclaimed social intentions, hand in hand with a dazzling progress in technology. And all of a sudden it found itself in its present state of weakness.
>
> This means that the mistake must be at the root, at the very foundations of thought in modern times. I refer to *the prevailing Western view of the world* which was born in the Renaissance and has found political expression since the Age of Enlightenment.[22]

Clearly, Solzhenitsyn is referring to what I am calling the MWM. He identifies this mind-set as "rationalistic humanism or humanistic autonomy: the proclaimed and practiced *autonomy of man from any higher force* above him."[h] If superior forces are not allowed—current epistemology has no way to register them, I have argued—

---

[h] Ibid., pp. 47–49; emphasis added. "It could also be called anthropocentricity," he adds, "with man seen as the center of it all" (p. 49).

On the day that I found myself writing these lines a letter reached me from a former student, Will Fitzhugh, relating an anecdote from his freshman philosophy course at Harvard University. It seems that when Emerson Hall (where the class met) was built, the Philosophy Department selected for the motto to be inscribed on its main wall, "Man is the measure of then human life has no alternative but to appear autonomous. If we are surprised to find Solzhenitsyn blaming this presumed autonomy for the fact that the Western world has lost its civic courage—"a fact which cannot be disputed is the weakening of human personality in the West," he tells us[23]—it is because, mechanists that we have largely and unconsciously become,[24] we assume that if superior forces exist they would tyrannize; we take their absence to be liberating. It seems not to occur to us that such forces might empower us. Submission (in Arabic, *Islam*) was the very name of the religion that surfaced through the Koran, yet its entry into history occasioned the greatest political explosion the world has known. If mention of this fact automatically triggers our fears of fanaticism, this simply shows us another defense our agnostic reflex has erected against the possibility of there being something that, better than we are in every respect, could infuse us with goodness as well as power were we open to the transfusion. It is usually said that the Copernican revolution humbled man by displacing him from the center of the universe, but this spatial dislodgment was nothing compared with the arrogance that followed in its wake, the arrogance of assuming that nothing exists that quite equals ourselves. For is it not we who ride the crest of evolution's advance? And what source of worth is there save evolution? For the MWM the question is rhetorical.

Mention of the individual and collective problems that the MWM abets has its place, but to seek a different outlook for the purpose of allaying them will not work. For this understandable (but in the end poorly conceived) motivation reinforces three assumptions of the very mind-set it seeks to replace.

The first of these is the assumption that history can be controlled. (That preoccupation with control again.) Do X, and Y will follow; adopt a different world view and a better world will result. Realistically there seems to be little evidence that history can be constructively controlled, though our destructive power might increase to the point where a madman could end it summarily.

---

all things." President Eliot, however, was of a different mind and what actually appeared was, "What is man that Thou art mindful of him?"

The occasion for the student's note to me was a return visit to his alma mater. He found that vines had obscured the inscription, leaving only three words visible, those words being "that Thou art," the claim (in its Vedantic formulation) that man is indissolubly joined to the Absolute. I shall return to that in section V, 4 below.

Working hand in glove with this assumption that history can be controlled is a second: the assumption that happiness can be bestowed. Heirs to any better world we might create would be happier than we are—this is what "better world" means—so in creating such a world we would hand happiness to those who are born into it. But this is not how life works. Comfort can be handed to us inasmuch as physical discomforts, at least, can be alleviated from without; if we are hungry food can be given us, if we are in pain, anodynes provided. Happiness, though, is different. Happiness cannot be bestowed from the outside or passively received from within. It must be won. It follows that it is impossible to do as much for another as one can do for oneself—save one's soul, for example, however one wishes to parse that phrase. If it sounds sanctimonious, it can be paired with its Zen variant: "No one can go to the bathroom for you."

The third dubious assumption underlying the "better world" rationale for a new outlook is the notion that truth is instrumental.[25] Here again the Prometheanism of modernity comes squarely to view: truth is seen as what will take us where we want to go. In the punchy formula of its distinctively modern, pragmatic definition, truth is what works. As a partial truth this is unexceptionable; the pragmatic attitude is an appropriate part of life, the yang part of its yin/yang whole—we were not born for idleness. But to make it the whole of life, and the version of truth it sponsors the whole of truth, is a trap so obvious that it took the bait of science's success to lure us into it. Truths in the plural are indeed instrumental; they can and should be chosen for ends we have in mind. But with truth in the singular—a person's or a people's final surmise as to the way things are—it is otherwise. Truth in this final, last-ditch sense is like love. If one loves for any reason save the beloved's intrinsic lovableness, it is not true love. Comparably, to hold X to be true for any reason save that in fact it is so is a contradiction in terms. Suppose that to the observation that "all men must die" the response were to be, "But surely that can't be true, for it makes people sad and fatalistic." To suspect that one is holding a belief for any reason save that it is true is instantly to undermine it.

"There is no right higher than that of the Truth," a maxim from India reminds us. It follows that we owe it to the truth to accept it;

metaphysics may not be moralized. Truth has no obligation to accommodate itself to us; it is we who must fashion ourselves to it. The appropriate reason for changing our outlook is not to create a better world or save the one we have. It is to see more clearly things as they are. All other considerations are secondary.

III. THE APPROACH TO A REVISED OUTLOOK THROUGH LOGIC

Kilimanjaro is the highest mountain in Africa. A number of years ago, as Hemingway noted in the epigraph to "The Snows of Kilimanjaro," the frozen carcass of a mountain leopard was found near its 19,565 foot snow-clad summit. No one seems to know what it was doing at that altitude.

Perhaps it was curious. We have seen that no prudential reason for changing our mind-set will do; in the end we must want a better one solely for the more accurate view it affords. But how can an improved outlook be acquired? To move from captivity toward a freedom we have yet to understand may be the most difficult task the mind can set for itself.

Let us begin with purely logical possibilities. Being no more than possibilities these will not persuade—that they are possible does not mean that they are true. But even to entertain alternatives to the MWM is a step toward loosening its hold on us, and if we can show that they are not inherently unreasonable, this will be an even longer step. It is as if, faced with a stake that has been driven deep into the ground, we begin in this section to rock it back and forth to loosen the hard earth around it. Not until the next section will we try to pull it up.

In section one we saw that exercise of newly discovered ways of controlling nature established an epistemology that produced the MWM. It follows that if we were to approach the world with intent other than to control it, it would show us a different guise. The opposite of the will-to-control is the wish to participate—a genuine desire to accent embracing yin over abrasive yang so that domination will not preclude partnership or assertiveness stymie cooperation. Such an alternative starting point would generate a whole new sequence, which can be contrasted visually with that of the MWM as follows:

	The MWM	*Logical Alternative*
anthropology: ↑	alienation ↖	fulfillment ↗
ontology (world view): ↑	naturalism ↖	transcendence ↗
epistemology: ↑	empiricism ↖	intuitive discernment ↗
motivation:	control	participation

The payoff of the revised starting point would be an ampler view of reality, and as it turns out to include things that are superior to us, "transcendence" is a fitting name for it. Its greater inclusiveness gives it a starting edge over the MWM, for the fact that every advance in science's understanding of nature has shown it to contain more than we had suspected suggests that a generous ontological vision, too, stands a better chance of being right than does a paltry one. But I leave that as no more than a passing observation. The trickiest link in the right-hand chain is its epistemology. Refusing to accept as truth's final arbiter the controlled experiment (or even objectivity, the consensus requirements of which push it relentlessly, as we have seen, toward sense-verificational empiricism), this alternate epistemology is faced with the problem of distinguishing between veridical discernments and ones that are deceptive. It is not within the scope of this essay to develop this alternative model systematically. I shall refer to it occasionally in what follows, but I introduce it mainly to limber up our imaginations—to keep them supple against an ossifying shell that threatens to become so strong that only the crowbar of historical events could break it.

There is another way to show that the MWM is not the only way to look at the world. Even if we accept the modern world's penchant for control we face a choice, for that road quickly forks. Control over what—the world or ourselves? More than once before I have referred to Ernest Gellner's report that for the MWM knowledge must be "effective" if it is to qualify as "genuine" (see again p. 77 above). But effective for what? For changing the objective, external world, or things within ourselves—the dispositions and predilections that constitute our characters and make us the persons we are? As self-transformation was not what interested the founding fathers of the MWM—Bacon's "knowledge is power" was not aimed at power for self-improvement—this mind-set has not proved to be sophisticated in handling this side of the question. It does not have a great deal to say on how we might break out of our self-centeredness and relate lovingly to the world at large. Secretly, it may wonder if there is much to say on this topic; as evidence, note the inverse ratio between prestige and attention to self-change in academic departments of psychology as we pass from experimental and cognitive psychology to clinical psychology, then humanistic psychology, and then transpersonal psychology. When the MWM has its way completely, as in the deterministic behaviorism of B. F. Skinner, self-change is not even admitted as a possibility.

This has produced a paradox. Out of the practical side of our mouths we continue to urge people to exercise their freedom and take responsibility, fearing that if they do not our society may come apart at the seams; Solzhenitsyn is not alone in warning of "spiritual exhaustion." Meanwhile, out of the theoretical side of our mouths we serve notice on these attributes and place them in jeopardy. In the natural sciences where Skinner's model of man obviously falls and where Freud hoped his would eventually find its place, human beings are not free at all;[1] Heisenberg's indeterminacy principle has not made the slightest difference here. As for the social sciences, they remain dedicated to explaining human behavior in terms of stimuli that provoke it. (Is the victim the murdered man or the man who murdered him, the latter having been victimized by society?) Even in the humanities, according to the latest avant-garde literary movement, it is not man who speaks; rather, it is language and, beneath it, matter that speak through him—I am referring to Deconstructionism as headed by Derrida, Foucault, and the late Roland Barthes. Everywhere the individual subject is devalorized in favor of contexts that call the tunes and pull the strings. It is what comes our way that is accented, not what we do with it.

Living as we do in a civilization that prides itself on using everything at its disposal—its resources, its invention, every scrap of information its computers can deposit in their data banks—it is not idle to ask if our most valuable unused resource may not be the capacity of persons to recognize themselves as responsible agents;

---

[1] "The deeply rooted belief in psychic freedom and choice is quite unscientific and must give ground before the claims of a determinism which governs mental life" (Sigmund Freud, *General Introduction to Psychoanalysis* [New York: Liveright, 1935], p. 95).

selves who ask not that the world deliver things into their laps, but that it provide a matrix for their moral and spiritual development—structures on which character can climb if it resolves to do so. There is a knowledge that is effective for this kind of climbing, but like poetry in the MWM, it is an outcast knowledge. For as Allan Wheelis has written:

> Among the sophisticated, the use of the term "will power" has become the most unambiguous badge of naivete. . . . The unconscious is heir to the prestige of will. As one's fate formerly was determined by the will, now it is determined by the repressed mental life. Knowledgeable moderns put their backs to the couch and in so doing may fail to put their shoulders to the wheel. As will has been devalued, so has courage; for courage can exist only in the service of the will. . . . In our understanding of human nature we have gained determinism: lost determination.[26]

IV. FROM LOGIC TO IMAGERY

Logic can show us that if we were to approach the world with an eye to embracing rather than controlling it, or asking how it might school us rather than serve us, it would reveal a different guise. But what that guise would be it cannot say. For this latter report, insight is required. And insight, as David Bohm has noted,

> announces itself in mental images. Newton's conception of gravity and Einstein's notion of the constant speed of light came to them as perceptions, as images, not as hypotheses or conclusions drawn from logical deduction. Formal logic is secondary to insight [via images] and is never the source of new knowledge.[27]

To add a third example to the two Bohm mentions, the image of a randomly branching tree not only crystallized Darwin's theory of natural selection but guided him through his successive formulations of it. His notebooks show him drawing it repeatedly, lavishing on it a care for representation and detail that shows clearly his need to steep his mind in the image if he were to wring from it everything it had to offer.[28]

So I, too, reach for an image that picks up with our realization that there is a different world that awaits discovery and moves us toward picturing what that world might be like. The one I choose appears in a wise and beautiful book by Gai Eaton, *The King of the Castle,* (from which the opening sentence of my preface was also drawn) and I quote it in full.

> Let us imagine a summer landscape, bounded only by our limited vision but in truth unbounded; a landscape of hills and valleys, forests and rivers, but containing also every feature that an inventive mind might bring to thought. Let us suppose that somewhere in this measureless extension a child has been blowing bubbles for the sheer joy of seeing them carried on the breeze, catching the sunlight, drifting between earth and sky. And then let us compare all that we know of our world, the earth and what it contains, the sun, the moon and the stars, to one such bubble, a single one. It is there in our imagined landscape. It exists. But it is a very small thing, and in a few moments it is gone.
>
> This, at least, is one way of indicating the traditional or—taking the word in its widest sense—the religious view of our world and of how it is related to all that lies beyond it. Perhaps the image may be pursued a step further. The bubble's skin reflects what lies outside and is, at the same time, transparent. Those who live within may be aware of the landscape in quite different ways. Those whose sight is weak or untrained may still surmise its existence and, believing what they are told by others who see more clearly, have faith in it. Secondly, there are some who will perceive within the bubble itself reflections of what lies outside and begin to realise that everything within is neither more nor less than a reflection and has no existence in its own right. Thirdly, as by a miracle of sight, there will be a few for whom transparency is real and actual. Their vision pierces the thin membrane which to others seems opaque and, beyond faith, they see what is to be seen.[29]

The balance of this essay touches on several points this image raises, but before I proceed to them let me enter a covering observation. It is not possible to adjudicate between contending outlooks objectively, but it is possible to say which is the more interesting. And on this count Eaton's image wins over the MWM hands down, for it allows for everything in the latter and vastly more besides.

Specifically, it directs us toward a reality whose qualitative reaches outstrip what the MWM discerns in the way that the latter's quantitative features—the size of the universe it sees, and its other countable features—exceed what Ptolemy had in mind.

V. THE IMAGE EXPLORED

Remembering that we are tracking truth not for its practical consequences but for its intrinsic worth while expecting that each turn in the road will open onto vistas more interesting than the ones before, I proceed now to touch on five points latent in the image I have chosen as guide. The first relates to our ability to see beyond the obvious.

1. The Possibility of Certitude

Last spring I received a letter from a young man who had been reading the book in which the image I am working with appeared. "When at one point the author spoke of 'the inrush of the Real,'" he wrote, "I felt that happening to me."

This is an important experience. The word "inrush" implies confidence, while the capitalization of the word "Real" indicates that it pertains here to matters that are important.

There is no way that the MWM can validate both those points.[30] Karl Popper spoke for that mind-set when he opened a colloquium at M.I.T. several years ago by saying, "Were it not for science, the skeptics would win hands down." Humanists tend to concur. The Deconstructionists to whom I have already referred are the current elite in the humanities. The whole of their powerful artillery is aimed, ultimately, at the presumption that thought can amount to more than myth or ideology in the disparaging senses of these words. Reasons are rationalizations. In science we can verify hypotheses; elsewhere we must remain in doubt.

Meanwhile we must live, and this calls for choices and guidelines for making them, ones we consider dependable. It is no use to play games with oneself here, pretending that something is true while knowing that in all likelihood it is not,[31] but as I am trying to steer clear of prudential considerations I shall not dwell on this impasse. Time is better spent on why we think rationality drives toward skepticism, to see if we have that point straight.

There are times that visit us all when we feel at sea about everything. T. S. Eliot described them well when he wrote:

The circle of our understanding
Is a very restricted area.
Except for a limited number
Of strictly practical purposes
We do not know what we are doing;
And even, when you think of it,
We do not know much about thinking.
What is happening outside of the circle?
And what is the meaning of happening?
What ambush lies beyond the heather
And behind the Standing Stones?
Beyond the Heaviside Layer
And behind the smiling Moon?
And what is being done to us?
And what are we, and what are we doing?
To each and all of these questions
There is no conceivable answer.[32]

When these states come over us they must be respected: faced honestly and stayed with, to learn from them what we can. What is not required is the use of intelligence to glorify (and in certain versions of existentialism, romanticize) these states as if they constitute the acme of human authenticity rather than the mental counterpart of the common cold, or in severe instances the flu, to which we periodically succumb. To level the sharpest charge possible, the relentless championing of relativism, which in its cultural, historical, psychological, social, or existential form underlies all contemporary skepticism, is in the end naive.

Relativism sets out to reduce every kind of absoluteness to a relativity while making an illogical exception for its own case.[33] In effect, it declares it to be true that there is no such thing as truth; that it is absolutely true that only the relatively true exists. This is like saying that language does not exist, or writing that there is no such thing as script. Total relativism is an incoherent position. Its absurdity lies in its claim to be unique in escaping, as if by enchantment, from a relativity that is declared alone to be possible.

Relativism holds that one can never escape human subjectivity. If that were true, the statement itself would have no objective value; it would fall by its own verdict. It happens, however, that human beings are quite capable of breaking out of subjectivity; were we unable to do so we would not know what subjectivity is. A dog *is* enclosed in its subjectivity, the proof being that it is unaware of its condition, for, unlike a man or a woman, it does not possess the gift of objectivity.

If Freudian psychology declares that rationality is but a hypocritical cloak for repressed, unconscious drives, this statement falls under the same reproach; were Freudianism right on this point it would itself be no more than a front for id-inspired impulses. There is no need to run through the variations of relativism that arise from other versions of psychologizing, historicizing, sociologizing, or evolutionizing. Suffice it to say that few things are more absurd than to use the mind to accuse the mind, not just of some specific mistake but in its entirety. If we are able to doubt, this is because we know its opposite; the very notion of illusion proves our access to reality in some degree.

Our minds were made to know, and they "flourish"—no one has said this better than Aristotle—when they work meaningfully at that function. They need not be overweening nor claim omniscience; indeed, one of the important things they can know is their place. But that place exists, and it is not confined to the laboratory. To see, as E. F. Schumacher reminded us shortly before his death, that "only those questions which cannot be answered with [laboratory] 'precision' have any real significance"[34] is the first step toward knowledge about those questions themselves.

The most unnoticed reason for current skepticism is our assumption that earlier ages were mistaken. If their outlooks were erroneous, it stands to reason that ensuing eras will show ours to be mistaken too; so runs this argument, which is so taken for granted that it is seldom even voiced. But if we could see that our forebears were not mistaken—they erred in details, but not in their basic surmises, which were so much alike that in *Forgotten Truth* I referred to them as "the human unanimity"—a major impediment to confidence in our global understandings would be removed. The next step would be to separate the reliability of our knowledge from questions of omniscience, to counter the suspicion that if we cannot know everything, what we do know must be tainted. I need not know the position of San Francisco relative to everything in the universe, much less what space and position finally mean, to be certain that, given the present position of our planet's poles, it lies predominantly west of Syracuse. From such simple beginnings we should be able to go on to separate the relativities that should give us pause from ones that are irrelevant, or worse—like sand thrown in the face of desert pilgrims.

2. A True Infinite

I have spent the time I did on certitude because there is not a great deal of point in asking how we might understand things differently if we have little confidence in understanding generally. On what a revalidated understanding might encompass, I shall be brief. There is space to do little more than point out several possibilities the post-MWM might explore.

An over-the-shoulder glance at the road we have come gives the lay of the land. That the region of reality the MWM has mapped with virtual certainty—its physical domain—has proved to be incomparably more interesting than we had suspected gives us reason to think that comparable extravagance awaits our astonished discovery in its other regions as well. And as I see no better star to steer by—better either in what it promises or in reasons for adopting it—I proceed to sketch the contours of the most interesting world I can image.[j]

Eaton's soap bubbles floating in a stupendous landscape are again our guide. The entire universe the MWM knows—eight billion galaxies with over eight billion stars in each—is contained in one of those bubbles, so we pass now to the landscape that envelops them. It would be a mistake to approach that landscape quantitatively, as if its size were what mattered. Size is not irrelevant—vastness has a majesty of its own—but it is the qualitative features of the surround that the image dwells on: its hills and valleys, its forests and rivers, its sunlight and breezes, as these would show themselves not to a civil engineer or surveyor, but to an artist, a naturalist, or an awe-struck mountaineer.

The MWM has an awesome instrument to register the quantitative marvels of reality, but its qualitative spectrum it cannot

---

[j] I suspect that the approach I am following—my methodology if you will—is clear by now, but let me state it explicitly. In place of our usual tendency to begin with the accepted world and add to it only what collective evidence requires, I am asking if it would harm us to conjure the most interesting world we can and then drop from it what reason erases. There is some resemblance to Anselm's *credo ut intelligam*, "I believe in order to understand." Or as Wilfred Smith, using current idiom to get at what *credo* meant in the Middle Ages, paraphrases Anselm, "I get involved in order to understand."

track—not beyond the cutoff point of human experience. So it acknowledges no field or center of awareness—no intelligence, "heart," sensibility, whatever term one prefers—that exceeds ours in the way human consciousness exceeds that of minnows or zebras. Eaton's image challenges this myopia; those who are confined by this anthropocentrism, "this bubble's skin," are persons "whose sight is weak or untrained." Gazing on the landscape as a whole, an observer would doubtless delight in our bubble were he to notice it, but "it is a very small thing," besides which most of its beauty derives from the way it "reflects what is outside" and enhances the majesty of the latter by its contrasting smallness.

The environment in question, we are told, is "in truth unbounded," which is to say infinite. The word is important in the MWM, but only in the sense in which it is used in physics and mathematics. And as these disciplines are interested only in the way the concept applies to sets and numbers, it is not a true infinite they are occupied with. From a metaphysical standpoint a mathematical infinite is blatantly finite, for it disregards everything in the world save several of its most abstract features. Solzhenitsyn is right: "The concept of a *supreme complete entity*," one whose presence would "restrain our passions and irresponsibility," does not figure in the post-modern outlook.[35]

3. Downward Causation

In the image we are working with, everything in the bubble of our universe is the consequence of things superior to it. The bubble comes into being because a child wants it to, and its properties—the colors that glisten on its irridescent surface—are occasioned by the brighter colors in the world around it. Causation throughout is downward—from superior to inferior, from what is more to what is less.

The West has, of course, known a philosophy of this sort; Aristotle was the first to state it explicitly. "If anyone wishes to think philosophically, Aristotle is the teacher to begin with," a book at hand advises,[36] and it is especially appropriate to invoke him here because he was not overly other-wordly; it was nature that engrossed him, even as it does us. Yet attraction seemed to him a better model for causation than propulsion; things are lured more than they are driven.

Note to begin with how pleasing this sense of causation is, this notion that things move by being drawn toward what exceeds them and will fulfill them to the degree that they refashion themselves to its likeness. For Aristotle, the entire universe was thus animated. Everything reaches toward its better in the effort to acquire for itself its virtues, as tennis players seek out opponents who play better than they do, children are drawn to slightly older playmates, and dogs prefer human company to their own kind—everywhere the compelling lure of that which we instinctively admire because of its manifest superiority. Aristotle's universe is like a pyramid of magnets. Those on each tier are attracted to the tier above while being empowered by that tier to attract the magnets below them. At the apex stands the only completely actual reality there is, the divine Prime and Unmoved Mover.

Grounded (or stuck, as one is sometimes tempted to say) in the MWM, we cannot today endorse this vision as true, but if our blinders have not grown grotesque we can at least respect its grandeur. In the terms of our image, the thought of bubbles blown for a child's delight has far more charm than the explanation (accurate, of course, but sufficient?) that credits them to the viscous properties of molecules. Extended to the cosmos, the child's delight translates into *lila,* the Indian notion of all creation as God's play, but here the human domain is enough. It may not be diversionary simply to pause for a moment to experience how good the notion of "downward causation" (as I am calling this principle of persuasion from above) might feel. To have a model that inspires, that shows us what we would like to become, while at the same time infusing us with the strength needed to approximate it, is as important a condition as life affords.

It is also one that, ontologically speaking, the MWM precludes. There is no way that mind-set can allow the possibility that the universe might be ordered teleologically, in the fashion just described. For to announce again the leitmotif of this essay, the MWM is a conceptual balloon inflated by knowledge of the sort that facilitates control, and such knowledge is necessarily limited (as we have seen) to things that are inferior to us. Jacques Monod is so pertinent here that I shall quote him again: "The cornerstone of the scientific method is . . . the *systematic* denial . . . of final causes."[37] It should not escape us that such causes are not denied because they have been found *not* to exist; only because they have not been found *to* exist. But how could they have been so found when search for them is excluded on principle—"*systematic* denial" is Monod's term; even the emphasis is his. The unspoken, but in no wise obscure, reason for rejecting final causes out of hand is that every glance in their direction would divert us from the efficient causes the MWM is bent on getting its hand on.

It is all very clear, and also ironical. For if the only way we are permitted to account for ontological novelty—new things coming into being—is through antecedent inferiors, what is the logical terminus of this downspout that evolution converts into an upspout? We do not have to guess at the answer, for the leading philosopher of science of our generation has told us, having made it the cornerstone of his life's work. "The basic theme of Karl Popper's philosophy," his biographer and foremost expositor writes, "is that something can come from nothing.[38]

Quite apart from whether this notion has a shred of explanatory power, is it intuitively believable?

4. The Self/World Divide

In the mid-1970s a graduate student in psychology at New York University ran an experiment involving college undergraduates who were taking a six-week summer course in business law. Dividing them into two groups, he had both groups gaze at what looked like a blank screen for a minute or so before each class session. Four times in the course of that minute a momentary, tachistoscopic message appeared on the screen, but as its four microseconds duration was too brief for it to be recognized, all that the students consciously saw was a flicker of light. The messages that were flashed to the two groups differed; for the control group it was "People Are Walking," whereas the experimental group was treated to "Mommie and I Are One." The groups had been matched for grade-point average, but when the scores of the blindly marked final examination were tabulated, the "Mommie and I" group was found to have scored almost a full letter grade higher in the course than did the control group, the numerical averages being 90.4 percent and 82.7 percent respectively.[39]

Such is the increase in power and effectiveness that can accrue when one feels tuned to one's world, for the tachistoscopic message is presumed to activate an early and powerful level of consciousness where "Mommie" represented (and in that layer of consciousness still represents) the world at large. Some psychologists dispute this interpretation, insisting that the only way information can enter the nervous system is through the conscious mind, but if they are right, from whence comes the improved performances? As of this writing eight studies along the lines of the one described have been conducted, and whether the subjects were trying to lose weight, stop smoking, get good grades, or improve their mental health the results have been positive.[40] A book that summarizes the entire field of research is in press. It speaks so directly to this section of my paper that its title, *The Search for Oneness*,[41] could have served for my heading.

It hardly seems necessary to say more on this point. So much is self-evident that I feel I need only arrange the pieces.

a. No other culture in history has tried to live by an outlook that isolates the human species from its matrix to the degree that ours does. Whereas formerly men and women sensed themselves to be distinguished from the rest of reality by no more than a bubble's skin, a film so thin as to be transparent (to call again on Eaton's image), we now face the impermeable wall of Descartes's disjunction. Once he categorically isolated matter from mind, science was able to seize that matter like a fumbled football and run with it. The tracks it has left inscribe a cosmos which, as an earlier essay noted, is

> denuded of all humanly recognizable qualities; beauty and ugliness, love and hate, passion and fulfillment, salvation and damnation. . . . Such matters [have of course] remained existential realities of human life, [but] the scientific world view makes it illegitimate to speak of them as being "objectively" part of the world, forcing us instead to define such emotional experiences as "merely subjective" projections of people's inner lives. . . . All that which is basic to the specifically human [is] forced back upon the precincts of the "subjective" which, in turn, is pushed by the modern scientific view ever more into the province of dreams and illusions.[k]

---

[k] Manfred Stanley, "Beyond Progress: Three Post-Political Futures," in *Images of the Future*, ed. Robert Bundy (Buffalo: Prometheus Books, 1976), pp. 115–16. I have used this and the three quotations that follow in other essays, but enter them again because I have encountered no others, penned from within the MWM itself, that bring out the issues quite as crisply.

b. The consequence of this fateful divorce, so obvious that Professor Stanley refers to it as now "a Sunday-supplement commonplace," is

> a spiritual malaise that has come to be called alienation. . . .
> The world, once an "enchanted garden," to use Max Weber's
> memorable phrase, has now become disenchanted, deprived of
> purpose and direction, bereft—in these senses—of life itself.[42]

> The dehumanizing price [of this outlook] is that our identities,
> freedom, norms, are no longer underwritten by our vision and
> comprehension of things. On the contrary we are doomed to
> suffer from a tension between cognition [what we believe to be
> true] and identity [who we sense ourselves to be].[43]

c. We have not been drawn into this alienating outlook because it is true, but by historical choice or accident; specifically, this essay has argued, by the way Western civilization has responded to its invention of modern science.

> It was Kant' merit to see that this compulsion [to see things this
> way] is in us, not in things. It was Weber's to see that it is
> historically a specific kind of mind, not mind as such, which is
> subject to this compulsion.[44]

Here, more than on any other point considered in this paper, we may be beginning to see light at the end of the tunnel, for our ecological crisis is all but forcing us to reexamine the Cartesian premise we have built on for four hundred years. I bypass here the radical proposal, ventured by countercultural scientists like Frithjof Capra, that Mahayana Buddhism, which includes an important idealist component, provides the best philosophical model for quantum physics that is currently available, in favor of more modest suggestions that emanate from scientists who are more established. Gregory Bateson subtitled *Mind and Nature,* his last book, "A Necessary Unity"; and biologist Alex Comfort argues in his *I and That* that though the self-world (I/That) divide is to some extent inevitable, it can hypertrophy, and in our minds has done so. Finally, there is this suggestive statement by Lewis Thomas:

It may turn out that consciousness is a much more generalized mechanism, shared round not only among ourselves but with all the other conjoined things of the biosphere. Thus, since we are not, perhaps, so absolutely central, we may be able to get a look at it, but we will need a new technology for this kind of neurobiology; in which case we will find that we have a whole eternity of astonishment stretching out ahead of us. Always assuming, of course, that we're still here.[45]

5. We Have What We Need

Once, when it had become clear that the days of Suzuki Roshi, founder of the San Francisco Zen Center, were numbered, his dharma heir, Richard Baker, asked him in distress, "How will we manage without you?" The Roshi answered, "Never forget: Everything you need you already have." There is an echo of this in *The Autobiography of Malcom X*. Describing his prison conversion to Islam and the difficulty he had in getting knees to bend in prayer that till then had bent only to jimmy locks, Malcom remarks: "I was going through the hardest thing, also the greatest thing, for any human being to do; to accept that which is already within you, and around you."[46]

It is difficult to think of a presumption more foreign to the MWM than this one. In Eaton's image nothing turns on time, for the limitless landscape is there from the start, waiting to be seen by anyone who looks outside his bubble and adjusts his vision to the reaches that extend beyond it. In the MWM, however, the case is the opposite. There time is decisive. Buckminster Fuller refers to "our failed yesterday and our half-successful today." All eyes are on tomorrow.

Partisans of the MWM are quick to object that if the Roshi's claim were taken seriously it would cut the nerve of social concern. The objection leaves the Roshi's own energetic life an anomaly, but let that pass. Once in the course of a television interview on progress I asked Reinhold Niebuhr if relinquishing the dream of historical progress would de-fuse social action. He answered with a question of his own: "To take his work seriously, need a doctor believe that he is eradicating disease?" We are back at the point that was made in section two. All myths are tied to the Golden Age of their origin, and in the case of the MWM it was an age when technology seemed to be effecting historical progress. So the MWM continues this mystique, focusing on society rather than the individual (specifically, on what society might give the individual), and on the future rather than the present (on what society might provide individuals with tomorrow that it cannot provide today).

This is why in the context of the MWM the heading of this section sounds bizarre. If we think of what we need as a happiness that is handed to us by society, then to say that "we have what we need" is cruelly false, for our society obviously hands us no such thing. But that society can hand people happiness is an illusion that was earlier challenged. Whether it can provide individuals on average with more opportunity than it now does to work out their own salvation, I leave as an open question.

VI. CONCLUSION

Do I expect our outlook to change in the directions I have tried to imagine? Not soon, and never for everyone.

The first half of that answer needs no elaboration. It is obvious that the MWM is not about to collapse in the way an avalanche of snow periodically slides off a roof. Section one of this essay was given to showing how firmly entrenched it still is.

The second half of my answer, though, may seem enigmatic, so let me conclude by making it less so. To revert for a last time to Gai Eaton's image, let us recall that those who live within its child-blown balloon can be aware of its surrounding landscape in different ways. Some merely surmise its existence. Others recognize its reflections on their bubble's surface, while still others, having a talent for the long look, pierce with their vision the bubble's membrane, which to others is opaque, and see what is to be seen.

This is not an egalitarian picture, ranking persons as it does by their respective powers of sight. But then, who claims that at face value our world is egalitarian? Only in its hidden harmony, in the respect in which we can all work on our power to see, is there the prospect that we are alike.

If the wisdom of the ages is indeed wisdom and teaches us anything, it is that the outlook I have been reaching for is, details aside, the most advanced to which mind can aspire; it represents, we might say, the higher mathematics of the human spirit. Civilizations and cultures can encourage their peoples to advance in its direction, but to dream of an age wherein everyone would enter it lockstep would be to perpetuate one of the errors of the MWM itself, its excessively temporal view of historical progress.

> *Because I do not hope to turn again*
> *Because I do not hope*
> *Because I do not hope to turn.*[47]

If it is too much to hope that our Western outlook will turn concertedly in the directions I have noted, it is not too much to hope that it will encourage, more than it has in this century, those who may choose to do so.

NOTES

1. Huston Smith, "Excluded Knowledge: A Critique of the Modern Western Mind-set," *Teachers College Record* 80, no. 3 (February 1979): 419–54.
2. I am not overlooking the rational, mathematical component in science, but the crucial role of the controlled experiment gives empiricism the edge. One thinks of the opposition as fine a mind as Chomsky's faces because his "Cartesian" linguistics leans toward rationalism.
3. I do not know the author of this quatrain. It was chalked on the blackboard at a meeting of graduate students I attended last year.
4. Daniel Dennett, "Review of *The Self and Its Brain* by Karl Popper and John Eccles," *Journal of Philosophy* 76, no. 2 (February 1979): 97.
5. New York: Ballantine Books, 1978, p. 7.
6. Harold Morowitz, "Rediscovering the Mind," *Psychology Today* 14, no. 2 (August 1980): 14.
7. Francis Crick, *Of Molecules and Men* (Seattle: University of Washington Press, 1966).
8. Morowitz, "Rediscovering the Mind," p. 12.
9. Annette J. Smith, "Playing with Play: A Test Case of 'Ethocriticism,'" *Journal of Biological Structures* 1, no. 11 (1978): 199.
10. Jean Piaget, *Play, Dreams and Imitation in Childhood* (London: Routledge & Kegan Paul, 1951).
11. D. Elkins, ed., *Six Psychological Studies* (New York: Random House, 1967).
12. John Bowlby, *Attachment and Loss,* vol. 1 (New York: Basic Books, 1969), emphasis added.
13. "The emotions we feel, which in exceptional individuals may climax in total self-sacrifice, stem ultimately from hereditary units that were implanted by the favoring of relatives during a period of thousands of generations" (Edward O. Wilson, "Altruism," *Harvard Magazine,* November–December 1978).
14. Edward O. Wilson, *Sociobiology,* abr. ed. (Cambridge: Harvard University Press, 1980), p. 3.
15. Barbara Brown, *Supermind* (New York: Harper & Row, 1980), p. 199.
16. D. and C. Johnson, "Totally Discouraged: A Depressive Syndrome of the Dakota Sioux," *Transcultural Psychiatric Research Review,* no. 2 (1965): 141–43.

17. Anthony Marsella, "Depressive Experience and Disorder across Cultures," in *Handbook of Cross-Cultural Psychology*, ed. Harry Triandis and Jurgis Draguns, vol. 6 (Boston: Allyn & Bacon, 1980), p. 254. I am indebted to Kendra Smith for pointing me to the references in this section.

18. Ibid., p. 255.

19. Alexander Solzhenitsyn, published as *A World Split Apart* (New York: Harper & Row, 1978).

20. Ibid., p. 35.

21. Ibid., p. 5.

22. Ibid., p. 47; emphasis added.

23. Ibid., p. 35.

24. I refer the reader to what Gellner calls the "mechanistic insistence" of an epistemology that aims at power; see p. 77 above.

25. In *Computer Power and Human Reason: From Judgment to Calculation* (San Francisco: W. H. Freeman, 1976), Joseph Weisenbaum, another participant in the Woodstock Symposium, warns of "the imperialism of instrumental reason" in our time.

26. "Will and Psychoanalysis," *Journal of the American Psychoanalytic Association* 4, no. 2 (April 1956): 256.

27. Statement by David Bohm at the Woodstock Symposium, "Knowledge, Education, and Human Values," 1980.

28. See Howard E. Gruber, "Darwin's 'Tree of Nature' and Other Images of Wide Scope," in *On Aesthetics in Science*, ed. Judith Wechsler (Cambridge: M.I.T. Press, 1978).

Images figured prominently in the Woodstock Symposium. Peter Abbs followed David Bohm to argue the need for education "to restore the power of the living image, to confer on it a high epistemological status, to put it alongside concept as one of the key ways in which we symbolize and then come to know our world."

29. London: Bodley Head, 1977, pp. 11–12.

30. To Edward Norman's observation, quoted on p. 98 above, that "there is no doubt that in developed societies education has contributed to the decline of religious belief" Robert Bellah adds that the decline is not in religious belief only. "The deepest indictment of the university," he told the Woodstock Symposium, "is that it erodes belief" generally.

31. Sociobiology provides an instance of such game playing. On the one hand we are told that as human beings have been programmed by their evolutionary history to be incorrigible mythmakers, we require conceptual systems that engage our loyalties; while on the other, that these systems must "satisfy our urge for knowledge" (paraphrase of Edward O. Wilson, in *Religious Studies Review* 5, no. 2 [April 1980]: 102). Whether a conceptual system our knowledge tells us is a myth can engage our loyalties is never squarely faced.

32. T. S. Eliot, "The Family Reunion," in his *Complete Poems and Plays* (New York: Harcourt, Brace & World, 1971), p. 291.

33. Frithjof Schuon's essay "The Contradiction of Relativism" in his *Logic and Transcendence* (New York: Harper & Row, 1975) has helped me crystallize the thoughts I set down in the next several paragraphs.

34. E. F. Schumacher, *A Guide for the Perplexed* (New York: Harper & Row, 1977), p. 5.

35. Solzhenitsyn, *A World Split Apart*, p. 57; emphasis added.

36. Mortimer Adler, *Aristotle for Everybody* (New York: Bantam Books, 1980), p. 174.

37. Jacques Monod, *Chance and Necessity,* p. 21.

38. W. W. Bartley, III, in *The Philosophy of Karl Popper,* ed. Paul Schilpp (La Salle, Ill.: Open Court, 1974), 2:675.

39. K. Parker, "The Effects of Subliminal Merging Stimuli on the Academic Performance of College Students," Ph.D. dissertation, New York University, 1977; reported in Lloyd Silverman, "Two Unconscious Fantasies and Mediators of Successful Psychotherapy," *Psychotherapy: Theory, Research and Practice* 16, no. 2 (Summer 1979): 220.

40. Lloyd Silverman, "A Comprehensive Report of Studies Using the Subliminal Psychodynamic Activation Method," issued by the New York Veterans Administration Regional Office and Research Center for Mental Health, New York University, 1980, p. 14.

41. L. H. Silverman, F. Lachman, and R. Milich, *The Search for Oneness* (New York: International Universities Press, in press). I am indebted to a former student, Robert Ebert, for calling my attention to the whole matter.

42. Manfred Stanley. Reference is on p. 55.

43. Gellner, *The Legitimation of Belief,* p. 207.

44. Ibid., pp. 206–7.

45. Lewis Thomas, *The Medusa and the Snail* (New York: Viking Press, 1979), p. 87.

46. Malcolm X, *The Autobiography of Malcolm X* (New York: Grove Press, 1964), p. 164.

47. T. S. Eliot, "Ash Wednesday," in his *Complete Poems and Plays,* p. 60.

·9·

CHECK POINTS

The carapace of scientism that has more or less imprisoned our century—"grabbed it by the throat" is Nobel laureate Elias Canetti's metaphor—is showing signs of cracking. Some of the fine lines that tell of possible fissures are on its nether side, and if these widen they will admit demonic forces of terrifying proportions. But while a world survives, it exhibits providentially a modicum of equilibrium that makes that survival possible. In our case this means that there are tracer-lines on the "ceiling" as well, and if it is these that open they will admit the light we need.

I have already said that I have no idea what *will* happen, but I do see places where things *might* happen. With respect to outlook, these show themselves either as weaknesses in the Post-Modern Mind that cannot indefinitely be patched or ignored, or as points of exceptional ferment occasioned by new evidence that does not fit existing theory. The present pages, which constitute an up-date of the previous essay, were written expressly for this book to identify four conceptual "hot spots" that deserve special attention. It will be wise to keep close watch on them, for if socio-political developments do not wrench us out of our current mind-set, it is likely to be shifts in these regions that will suggest a new paradigm.

Of the four places I shall point to where the Post-Modern Mind shows signs of weakening, two are occasioned by stress and two by distress. Stress refers to the strain this mind is experiencing in trying to accommodate new data in science; distress to the pain in our time that prevailing assumptions unconsciously exacerbate. I shall deal with distress first, under the headings of reductionism and reason, and then turn to the stress that is building up in evolutionary theory and frontier physics.

1. *Distress stemming from reductionism.* In a letter to the London *Times,* Valerie Eliot, T. S. Eliot's widow, once wrote:

> My husband, T. S. Eliot, loved to recount how late one evening he stopped a taxi. As he got in the driver said: "You're T. S. Eliot." When asked how he knew, he replied: "Ah, I've got an eye for a celebrity. Only the other evening I picked up Bertrand Russell, and I said to him, 'Well, Lord Russell, what's it all about,' and do you know, he couldn't tell me."

Reticence in the face of the All is appropriate, but I intend to speak at a more proximate level and, with apologies for profaning the dead, to use Russell as a foil to point to the first place where the Post-Modern Mind shows signs of buckling. Believing as Russell did that "what science cannot tell us, mankind cannot know," it is not surprising that he had little to say to the cabbie's question; for on existential, global, and value questions science has, in the end, nothing to say (see pp. 66–67 and 111–12 above).

Yet we give the scientific method pride of place in our noetic repertoire, with the not surprising consequence that our values are in shambles. Rebecca West is considered by many to be the best reporter of our century, and when Bill Moyers recently asked her to identify "the mood of the day," she answered, "A desperate search for a pattern."[1] If the desperation increases, it may force us to ask whether we want to continue to place power over nature ahead of how we should live in our noetic program. For as we have seen (the diagram on p. 144 above epitomizes the point), far from being a photograph of the way things are, the current Western worldview is a painting—an expressionistic painting that projects on an external canvas a display of our will to control. "Here I sell what everyone wants—power," Matthew Bolton (James Watt's partner) posted on the wall of his machine shop. He knew his market. To an extent we are only now coming to realize, the West bought.

A university president is worth listening to here, for the claims of knowledge and values (the first represented by the university, the second by the needs of society) reach his ears in almost equal proportions. In an interview for *U.S. News and World Report,* 10 November 1980, Steven Muller of The Johns Hopkins University identified the "Hegelian contradiction" I am pointing to with syllogistic precision. Beginning by noting that "the biggest failing in higher education today is that we don't provide a value framework," he moved surgically to the cause: "This situation has come about because the modern university is rooted in the scientific method [which] doesn't provide a value system."

"It has taken a long time for that to become apparent," Muller points out, "because our traditional value system survived intact for such a long time." But now that its force is spent—"all our institutions have lost a coherent set of values"—we see that science cannot *re*place what it has unintentionally *dis*placed. The consequence that Muller sees for the university is that it is "turning out skilled barbarians." He does not go on to draw the moral I did two paragraphs above, but his analysis clearly points in its direction: we may not be able to continue much longer without asking ourselves explicitly whether we want to rely as disproportionately on scientific knowing as the Post-Modern Mind has and does. That the scientific method should have an important *place* in the university goes without saying. But for the university to be "rooted" in that method (Muller's assessment) is for it to assert, whether intentionally or not, that we continue to value power over nature more than we value wisdom—power which, one cannot resist adding, can be misused whereas wisdom cannot be.

This needs further consideration. In a way, Muller's diagnosis, for all its accuracy, is unavailing since it produces no prescription: "The trouble," he admits, "is we don't know where we are going to get" the coherence and values we need. But between seeing a problem and not knowing its answer there is an intermediate possibility: that we might at least come to see what it is in our present stance that *keeps* us from seeing the answer; namely, (in this case) our having filled our noetic horizon with a way of knowing that is value-incompetent.[a]

---

[a] "Filled our horizon" will be challenged as being an overstatement; it will be protested that every scientist who is at all reflective knows that there are things his science cannot get at. But quite apart from whether we *laymen* see this even if scientists do, two points must be made. To the phrase "cannot get at," many scientists add, under their breath, the word "yet," thereby bolstering again the faith that *eventually* science will save us. And second, even if we saw clearly that science can *never* provide the value help we need, it would not follow that there is an alternative epistemology that could succeed where science fails. As an ascientific, value-effective epistemology is not on the Post-Modern Mind's agenda, to say that science's epistemology "fills its horizon" is not an exaggeration.

There are signs that this intermediate point is at last being recognized, which, coupled to the urgency of our value needs, is my reason for citing this as one of the points where the Post-Modern Mind may "give." Of Aristotle's (still useful) four divisions of nature—mineral, vegetable, animal, and human—science deals effectively with only the lower ones, and adequately with only the lowest one. The differences between inanimate and animate, plant and animal, and animal and human, are so momentous that it makes more sense intuitively to recognize that different qualities, powers, and even substances are involved, not just different processes, as reductionists would like us to believe. Reductionists love the word "process" because, like "systems," it allows them to try to account for differences in kind as if they were only differences in degree—degree of complexity or patterned arrangement. In ascending from inanimate to animate, and on to consciousness and self-awareness, no new *things* need be acknowledged, they argue, only new arrangements of things that were present all along. (Is no one going to laugh, one wonders, once the claim is stripped to its bare simplicity?) The postulate so ill accords with our direct experience that only scientific triumphalism[b] could have induced us to discount that experience as long as we have. Scientists abjure talk of a life-force because they cannot get at it; if it exists it is invisible and does not connect with their instruments. Yet the difference between life and death remains, and it increases in quantum leaps as consciousness and self-awareness are added. The holy, eerie dread we feel in the presence of a corpse differs *in kind* from our response to a watch that has run down. In the watch every *thing* that was present *remains* present, whereas in the corpse something crucial and mysteriously different has departed. The same must be said of the difference consciousness adds to life that is without it: a dog knocked unconscious by a car clearly lacks something it had the moment before, something that phrases like "distinctive patterns of neural circuitry" divert our attention from. To say that an animal is a physio-chemical system of immense complexity is perfectly true, but it takes no account of the "animalness" of the animal. Similarly, when the difference between consciousness and self-awareness is

---

[b] Faith that, given time, science has all the answers, or at least all that will be forthcoming; hence, that science will save us if anything can.

slurred, vast energies are directed to the study of animals in the hope that this will contribute to the understanding of human beings. This is like studying physics in the hope of learning biology. Since higher forms *contain* the lower, something about the higher can indeed be learned from studying the lower—everything, in fact, *except what makes it higher.* To think of human beings as "naked apes" bespeaks an entire approach, one that turns its back on man's distinctive essence. It is as if it were suddenly to occur to dogs that they might get further if they thought of themselves as "barking cabbages."

The situation invites such satire, which in this instance is drawn from E. F. Schumacher's *A Guide for the Perplexed.* In that book the author arranges Aristotle's "four kingdoms" in an inverted pyramid that reads from the bottom up as follows:

human: matter + life + consciousness + SELF-AWARENESS
animal: matter + life + CONSCIOUSNESS
plant: matter + LIFE
MATTER

The capitalized words with which each each line ends denote the different substances or powers I have spoken of. All of these save matter are invisible—no one has ever seen life or consciousness or self-awareness—and are therefore beyond the range of science, yet it is obviously in these higher registers that our lives are lived. Or better, as all our thoughts, emotions, feelings, imaginations, reveries, dreams, fantasies are woven of life, consciousness, and self-awareness, this latter triumverate is what we essentially *are.* And they are what values are as well,[c] we can add to get us back to the point with which this section is basically concerned. I have conceded along the way that science's inability to deal with values does not prove that a value-competent epistemology is possible. But we shall never know whether it is or not until we accord life, consciousness, and self-awareness autonomous status, meaning by this, *epistemologically,* that they must be understood in their own right, as having their own properties and principles which instruments tai-

[c] Actually the whole diremption of fact and value which Hume talked the modern mind into so that science could proceed without value encumbrances is a mistake. The subtleties that surround that philosophical error, though, place it outside the scope of this present short statement.

lored to other things cannot probe; and *ontologically,* that they do not depend on the physical bodies that sometimes "house" them. If this ontological point sounds radical in saying right out loud that there are things that are not only invisible but without material components entirely, it at least brings into the open how far postmodern ontology is removed from where it needs to be. For until the value domain is respected in the way that science respects nature, deeming it worthy of infinite attention, it is naive to think that values will show us their deep laws. And—this final point is the one that current value discussions have yet to take into account, as President Muller's otherwise admirable statement illustrates—this full respect will not be forthcoming until the value domain (which to physical eyes, remember, is invisible) is accorded autonomy on a par with that of nature.

Such ontic investiture is a long way off, but we do now have on our doorstep the realization that the value question can no longer be deferred, and that the premises of the Post-Modern Mind work against dealing with it adequately. The second half of this realization is cast in the negative, but even so, it opens the prospect of a new departure. To go back to Eliot and Russell, we are where Eliot found himself on reading Russell's "A Free Man's Worship." He is reported to have remarked, "It leaves me with no idea where truth lies, save that it must be in the opposite direction from here."

2. *Distress occasioned by reason.* Three epistemologies have dominated the West. Roughly speaking, they can be identified with Plato, Aristotle, and Bacon, and they differ in the instrument of knowledge—the noetic organ, we might call it—that they consider decisive. For Bacon it was the senses, for Aristotle reason, and for Plato the intuitive intellect.

Chronologically reversed, Bacon tagged "knowledge" to what helps man increase his power over nature. Turning his back on Aristotle's "first principles" which he thought were indemonstrable, Bacon narrowed knowing's focus to the discovery of what he called "middle axioms" or the laws of nature. As these come to light through observation and experimentation with sensible particulars, Bacon tied truth to inductions arrived at in "a certain way," the way of experiment or the method of "natural philosophy." Nothing deserves the credentials of truth that is not arrived at by this one useful and sovereign method. In augmenting the "kingdom of man," truth emerges as "utility" and knowledge as power. Bacon's importance derives from his unhesitating decision to ensconce these new definitions. When wisdom is equated with science, "sapience" consists in knowing what serves material interests.

Aristotle, too, thought knowledge should be objective and demonstrable, but in his case demonstration was achieved through logic rather than experiments that report to the senses. Induction from sense data can produce agreed-upon universals, he believed; and it is from these universals that the real work of knowing— proof, *apodeixis*—begins. For real knowledge is knowledge that logic discloses and undergirds. It is not surprising that Aristotle found it urgently necessary to work out and codify the rules of valid inference, a task he brilliantly executed in his *Analytics*. If Bacon is the classic empiricist, Aristotle is the classic rationalist.

And Plato the classic humanist, we can add to complete the triumverate, "humanist" being used to demonstrate his conviction that knowing draws on more of the self than its senses (Bacon), or even its senses and reason (Aristotle). In claiming agreement (inductively induceable self-evidence) for his first principles, Aristotle knew that he was departing from his teacher. He did so because he wanted certainty—knowledge that was objectively compelling for all rational minds—as much as Bacon wanted knowledge that was effective over nature. Plato too began by hoping for such certainty, but he came reluctantly to conclude that agreement could only be expected on matters of secondary importance. For in the things that matter most, everything turns on how much the knower sees. And seeing here involves intuitive discernment, the "eye of the soul" or intellect as Plato sometimes calls it,[2] whose powers are proportional to the moral stature the soul has attained (see pp. 52–53 above). Courage, justice, and temperance are noetic aids. Bacon said knowledge is power. Faithful to his teacher Socrates, Plato said it is virtue.

In summary: Plato saw knowledge as deriving from intellect, reason, and the senses; Aristotle, from reason and the senses; Bacon, from the senses only, almost. The progressive constrictions are dramatic.

What has all this to do with distress? The preceding section noted that the distress in question relates to value uncertainties, and that science is helpless to relieve them. Once this is seen, reason presents itself as the next resource to call on: Are we not rational beings?—

let reason tell us how to live. But Bacon's sense-preempted reason is virtually identical with value-incompetent science, and the Post-Modern Mind has no place for Plato's intellect. This leaves Aristotle's logic-oriented reason as the only candidate. But the "first principles" from which Aristotle himself reasoned have long since collapsed, and there is growing uncertainty as to whether the logic that is his remaining legacy can get much further with value questions than science can. For deprived of both Aristotelian "first principles" and the special insights of Plato's intellect, logic has nothing but ordinary, everyday experience with which to begin (see pp. 53–54 above). And beginning there, it must end there too, it would seem, for in itself it has no wings. There is plenty of logical reasoning in the university outside of the sciences—in the social sciences, philosophy, and the humanities. President Muller knows this well, but he obviously saw no hope there.

So his conclusion stands: "We don't know where we are going to get" the value coherence we need. As that need increases, something in our present lineup, it would seem, will have to change. The issues are joined at points that make it likely that the change could occur in the way the three great epistemologies of the West are currently "gestalted."

3. *Stress in evolutionary theory.* Turning from human distress to the stress that prevailing scientific paradigms are experiencing as a result of new data and other considerations they must face, I begin with the most influential teaching of the modern age, the theory of evolution, leading into it with an anecdote. Once when M.I.T. philosophers were playing the game "Which philosopher delivers most truth per page?," I was surprised to hear James Thompson nominate the Scottish philosopher of common sense, Thomas Reid. Several years later, finding that Keith Lehrer had written his doctoral dissertation on Reid, I asked him if Thompson's choice surprised him. He said it did, but in a few minutes returned to the point. "If you replace 'God' with 'Evolution' in Reid's works," he said, "Thompson comes close to being right."

The Post-Modern Mind virtually *has* replaced God with evolution as man's creator. That we have become thereby "Children of a Lesser God," to invoke the title of a current Broadway play, is (though true) not the reason for bringing up the subject here. I do so to show this as another area where a break-through seems imminent. I have already mentioned the Gaia Hypothesis (pp. 43–44 above). Here I shall focus on rumblings in the very foundations of evolutionary theory.

It's quite simple, really. As *description*—the fossil record, which is to say the age and continuities/discontinuities in life-forms that that record discloses—evolution is true and the Creationists mistaken. But as *explanation,* neo-Darwinism is a failure, and one that has serious psychological repercussions. This crucial distinction is not being drawn today. As a result, we witness a shouting match between the scientific establishment and fundamentalists, each of which has hold of a half-truth and, by the same token, is partially in error.

Neo-Darwinism is not a description of life's journey on this planet; it is a theory that purports to explain that journey. Specifically, it claims that natural selection working on chance mutations accounts for what has occurred. The reason for predicting that something is going to change in the theory is the growing realization that the first of these terms, natural selection, is a tautology, while the other, chance mutations, points to something that is inexplicable. A theory that claims to explain while standing with one foot on a tautology and the other in an explanatory void, is in trouble.

First, natural selection. It argues that the pressure of populations on environments results in the survival of the fittest. But as no criterion for "fittest" has been found to be workable other than "that which survives," the theory is circular. As the late Professor Waddington wrote: "Survival . . . denotes nothing more than leaving most offspring. The general principle of natural selection . . . merely amounts to the statement that the individuals which leave most offspring are those which leave most offspring. It is a tautology."[3]

Now chance mutations. Chance is the opposite of having a cause; something that happens by chance admits to no reason or purpose for its occurrence. In using the word, it is politically important for scientists to reinforce this popular understanding, for if this is in any way a purposive universe, that aspect of it is beyond science's ken, and its votaries become demoted to partial knowers.[d] Once again

---

[d] Wishing to keep the discussion clean for cognitive considerations, I have tried in these essays to steer clear of political factors that shaped the modern and post-modern minds. In

let me quote Jacques Monod: "The cornerstone of scientific method is . . . the *systematic* denial that 'true' knowledge can be got at by interpreting phenomena in terms of . . . 'purpose'" (emphasis his; see pp. 67 and 112 above). The determination with which evolutionists insist that chance be read as the opposite of purpose can be seen in the way they speak of "blind" and "pure" chance when there are no such things in science itself: in science chance is a number. There is, however, another way of viewing chance; namely, as an occurrence whose cause lies outside the world of discourse in which the occurrence is considered. If a bird found birdseed sprinkled on the snow only when a forest ranger passed its way and the ranger came only at night while the bird was asleep, it would doubtless credit the seed as "due to" chance. (Note the way "due to" seems to produce a cause where none is offered.) By this second reading, the combination of chance and necessity—random mutations joined to natural selection—"is precisely just the necessary and sufficient condition required for any who would wish to assert that the evolutionary process is . . . purposive,"[4] be they animists, vitalists, teleologists of any stripe, or classical theists—Hegel, Bergson, Whitehead, Polanyi, Teilhard de Chardin, whoever.

"The introduction of probability [as the specification of chance's perimeters] into scientific description constitutes the one case in which *science expressly renounces an explanation in terms of natural causes*" (ibid., p. 438). But evolutionary theory then faces the statistical *improbabilities* that pepper life's ascent. It used to be argued that geological ages are so interminable as to allow time for anything and everything to happen. The notion required getting used to, but as long as it was thought of in single numbers, analogous to the number 26, say, turning up on a roulette wheel exactly when it was needed in a given evolutionary thrust, it could be accepted. We now see, though, that significant organic changes require that innumerable component developments occur *simultaneously* and *independently,* in bones, nerves, muscles, arteries, and the like.

allowing the word "political" to enter the above sentence I have slipped from this resolve, and having done so will let an able historian of science tell the story in a single sentence: "Naturalism was above all the weapon of the newly rising group of 'professionalised' scientists, struggling to wrest cultural power—influence over education, for example—from an older elite that in most European countries was closely identified with the institutional Church" (Martin Rudwick, "Senses of the Natural World and Senses of God: Another Look at the Historical Relation of Science and Religion," in M. B. Hesse and A. R. Peacocke [eds.], *The Sciences and Theology in the Twentieth Century* [London: Routledge & Kegan Paul, in press]).

This escalated the demand on probability theory astronomically, like having 26 come up simultaneously on ten or fifteen tables in the same casino, followed by all the tables reporting 27, 28, and 29 in lock-step progression. The number of generations through which a large number of immediately disadvantageous variations would have had to persist to turn reptiles into birds, say—scales into feathers, solid bones into hollow tubes, the dispersion of air sacs into various parts of the body, the development of the shoulder muscles and bones to athletic proportions, to say nothing of conversion to a totally different biochemistry of elimination and the changeover from coldblooded to warm—makes the notion of raw chance preposterous. As Professor Pierre Grassé, who for thirty years held the chair for evolution at the Sorbonne, has written:

> The probability of dust carried by the wind reproducing Dürer's "Melancholia" is less infinitesimal than the probability of copy errors in the DNA molecules leading to the formation of the eye; besides, these errors had *no relationship whatsoever* with the function that the eye would have to perform or was starting to perform. There is no law against daydreaming, but science must not indulge in it.[5]

If we want to stay with chance, obviously something is going to have to intervene to reduce it to conceivable bounds. This is where the search goes on now; vocabularies proliferate with repressor genes, co-repressor and apo-repressor, modifier and switch genes, operator genes that activate other genes, cistrons and operons that constitute sub-systems of interacting genes—even genes that regulate the rate of mutations in genes. Anything to narrow unlimited chance to chance within conceivable proportions. On a different front, with the displacement of Darwin's gradualism with the "punctuational" model, it is now conceded that the "missing links" between most species will not be found. It happened too fast. "Most change has taken place so rapidly and in such confined geographic areas that it is simply not documented by our imperfect fossil record."[6]

From *The New Encyclopedia Britannica,* which can be taken as summarizing intellectual orthodoxy at the time of its publication in 1975, one would gather that neo-Darwinian theory is as settled as

Newtonian. It tells us that "evolution is accepted by all biologists and natural selection is recognized as its cause. . . . Objections . . . have come from theological and, for a time, from political standpoints" (vol. 7, p. 23). Who would suspect from this that biologists of the stature of Ludwig von Bertalanffy have been writing: "I think the fact that a theory so vague, so insufficiently verifiable and so far from the criteria otherwise applied in 'hard' science, has become a dogma, can only be explained on sociological grounds"? Or that Sir Karl Popper hailed Norman Macbeth's highly critical *Darwin Retried* as a "most meritorious and really important contribution to the debate?" Or that Arthur Koestler's investigation into the subject led him to conclude that neo-Darwinism is a citadel in ruins?[e] Or that recently the "Nova" program on PBS raised the question "Did Darwin Get It Wrong?," with the announcement reading, *"The Origin of Species* is challenged with new facts and new emotion"?

Though I have clearly shown my hand in these paragraphs, my intent has not been to argue the issues that are at stake but rather to "flag" them as places where changes are afoot and likely to accelerate. It is also a place where social pressures, in the act of buttressing certain errors, are forcing others into the open. I refer to the Creationists who at the moment have bills before seventeen state legislatures. Thinking it important to believe that the earth is only a few thousand years old, their alternative scenario for life's ascent is mistaken, but in challenging neo-Darwinism's unsuccessful mechanistic explanation of that ascent, they are performing a public service.[f] *The New Encyclopedia Britannica* article that I have cited tells us that "Darwin did two things; he showed that evolution was in fact contradicting scriptural legends of creation and that its cause, natural selection, was automatic with no room for divine guidance or design" (p. 23). Do biologists really want to take on issues like "creation," "divine guidance," and "divine design"? Implicitly where not explicitly, they have (since Darwin) done so. It is time that

---

[e] "One of the crumbling citadels of orthodoxy . . . is the neo-Darwinian theory of evolution" (*Janus: A Summing Up* [New York: Vintage Books, 1978], p. 166). Koestler compares Jacques Monod's *Chance and Necessity* to Custer's Last Stand, and repeats, "the citadel they are defending lies in ruins" (p. 192).
[f] Even the American Civil Liberties Union is confused here. Instead of winnowing the Creationist's claims, it rejects them *in toto*, assuming that *their* liberties are not being infringed because only scientific truth is arrayed against them.

they come clean and tell us if their negative conclusions are integral to evolutionary theory. In this one (totally unprecedented?) case, are metaphysical and theological imponderables settled by positive fact? Martin Lings is probably right in writing that "more cases of loss of religious faith are to be traced to the theory of evolution . . . than to anything else."[7]

4. *Stress in frontier physics.* That identical twins look alike doesn't really surprise us, for we know they have matured from identical genes. But if we were to separate a pair of such twins, situating one in New York, let us say, and the other in New Zealand, and then find that when the New Yorker cocks his head to the left the New Zealander regularly and *simultaneously* cocks his to the right, we would be more than surprised. We would be astounded. Yet this is the way nature can behave, apparently. The twins are only an analogy scientists invoke for the benefit of those of us who have difficulties with notions like the intrinsic angular momentum of particles, or their spin. Each particle in a pair that is created and then separated seems to know instantaneously what is happening to the other. The Einstein-Podolsky-Rosen experiment brought this to attention. Bell's Theorem formalized its results.

Physics continues to be grounded in the principle that no physical interactions can exceed the speed of light. But the experiment just named, and a dozen or so more along the same lines, blatantly violate that principle.

David Bohm thinks that connections of the sort described, ones that fly in the face of space-time separations, suggest that the nature we know derives from an "implicate order" that is "whole" in a way its derivatives are not, a way that we do not presently understand. To provide an intuitive sense of the matter he suggests the following device:

> Let us begin with a rectangular tank full of water, with transparent walls (see figure below). Suppose further that there are two television cameras, A and B, directed at what is going on in the water (e.g., fish swimming around) as seen through the two walls at right angles to each other. Now let the corresponding television images be made visible on screens A and B in another room. What we will see there is a certain *relationship* between the images appearing on the two screens. For example, on

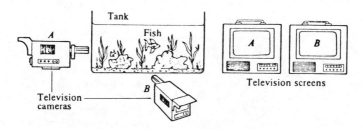

screen A we may see an image of a fish, and on screen B we will see another such image. At any given moment each image will generally *look* different from the other. Nevertheless the differences will be related, in the sense that when one image is seen to execute certain movements, the other will be seen to execute corresponding movements. Moreover, content that is mainly on one screen will pass into the other, and vice versa (e.g., when a fish initially facing camera A turns through a right angle, the image that was on A is now to be found on B). Thus at all times the image content on the other screen will correlate with and reflect that of the other.

Of course, we know that the two images do not refer to independently existent though interacting actualities (in which, for example, one image could be said to 'cause' related changes in the other). Rather, they refer to a single actuality, which is the common ground of both (and this explains the correlation of images without the assumption that they causally affect each other). This actuality is of higher dimensionality than are the separate images on the screens; or, to put it differently, the images on the screens are two-dimensional *projections* (or facets) of a three-dimensional reality. In some sense this three-dimensional reality holds these two-dimensional projections within it. Yet, since these projections exist only as abstractions, the three-dimensional reality *is* neither of these, but rather it is something else, something of a nature beyond both.[8]

What Bohm is proposing is that the atemporal and seemingly noncausal connections of particles with one another may be understood through an extension of the notion he has described. But what is the added-dimensional, super-integrated implicate order his fish tank symbolizes?

It is an interesting time to be alive.

NOTES

1. "A Visit with Dame Rebecca," on "Bill Moyers' Journal," 8 July 1981.

2. For direct apprehension of the highest modes of being, "Plato frequently [uses the word] 'intellection' (*noesis*) as distinguished from discursive reason or understanding (*dianoia*) which proceeds through deduction or inference" (Robert Cushman, *Therapeia* [Chapel Hill: University of North Carolina Press, 1958], p. 81).

3. C. H. Waddington, *The Strategy of the Genes* (London: Allen and Unwin, 1957), pp. 64–65.

4. William Pollard, "A Critique of Jacques Monod's *Chance and Necessity*," *Soundings*, Winter 1973, pp. 435–36. As a physicist who for many years directed the Oak Ridge Project, Dr. Pollard has worked with the concept of chance in quantum mechanics his entire professional life. Perhaps it is also because he is a priest of the Episcopal Church that he has been able to see the interface between chance and purpose with singular clarity. See footnote j in chapter 6, above.

5. *Evolution of Living Organisms: Evidence for a New Theory of Transformation* (New York: Academic Press, 1977), p. 104.

6. Steven Stanley, "Darwin Done Over," *The Sciences*, October 1981, p. 19.

7. *Studies in Comparative Religion* 4, no. 1 (Winter 1970): 59.

8. David Bohm, *Wholeness and the Implicate Order* (London: Routledge and Kegan Paul, 1980), pp. 187–88.

·10·

THE SACRED UNCONSCIOUS*

More than once I have foresworn prophecy; the preceding essay points to places where breakthroughs *may* occur, not necessarily *will* occur. There are times, though, when to act as if something *has* happened helps it *to* happen, and this next statement adopts this approach. Taking the human self as its object, it describes that self "from the further shore," as Buddhists would say.

There is need to see it in that light, for the view from this shore does not do us justice; as Saul Bellow points out in the Nobel Lecture I have already quoted, "we do not think well of ourselves." The complete edition of the works of Sigmund Freud contains over four hundred entries for neurosis and none for health, and even if we bracket pathology, what account of ourselves is given by psychologists, sociologists, historians, journalists, and writers? "In a kind of contractual daylight," Bellow continues,

> they see [us] in the ways with which we are so desperately familiar. These images of contractual daylight, so boring to us all, originate in the contemporary world view. We put into our books the consumer, civil servant, football fan, lover, television viewer. And in the contractual daylight version their life is a kind of death. There is another life, coming from an insistent sense of what we are, that denies these daylight formulations and the false life—the death in life—they make for us. For it is false, and we know it, and our secret and incoherent resistance to it cannot stop, for that resistance arises from persistent intuitions. Perhaps humankind cannot bear too much reality, but neither can it bear too much unreality, too much abuse of truth.

---

* Reprinted with negligible changes from Roger Walsh and Dean Shapiro (eds.), *Beyond Health and Normality: The Exploration of Extreme Psychological Well-Being* (New York: Van Nostrand Reinhold, 1982).

Two psychiatrists, dissatisfied with the current model of the self, have brought together a book that challenges its "desparately familiar . . . boring. . . false" self-estimate. It includes this essay as my contribution to their venture.

In *The Next Million Years,* a book published around the time of Darwin's centennial, his grandson, Charles Galton Darwin, considered the prospects for genetic engineering. Writing as a geneticist, he concluded that the difficulties were formidable but solvable. What was not solvable, he thought, was the goal of such engineering—agreement as to the kind of person we would like to produce. Nietzsche and Van Gogh were geniuses but went mad— would we want their genes in our gene pool? It's a good question. It makes us see the nerve of a book that tries to define the highest good for man.

Writing as a philosopher and historian of religions, let me venture my perception of this "human best" as follows. If Marx unmasked our social unconscious and Freud our personal unconscious, both piercing through superstructures, or rather substructures, that hide true causes and motives, the supreme human opportunity is to strike deeper still and become aware of the "sacred unconscious" that forms the bottom line of our selfhood.

I shall not go into reasons for assuming that this final unconscious exists; I have discussed some of them in my *Forgotten Truth* where I use the word "spirit" for what I am here calling the sacred unconscious. Nor will I map here our human consciousness to show the relation of this deepest level to ones that are more proximate; that I attempted in the chapter on "The Levels of Selfhood" in the book just mentioned. Instead I shall try to surmise what our lives would be like if our deepest unconscious were directly available to us. What would a supremely realized human being, here conceived as one that is consciously aware of his or her sacred unconscious, be like? How would such a person look to others and feel to him/herself?

It is easier to say what s-he would not be like than to picture him or her positively, as the "tragic flaw" theory of art reminds us. No writer would dream of trying to create a perfect hero; he would sense instinctively that such a figure would seem completely fictitious—a cardboard cutout. But let the author endow an otherwise strong character with a tragic weakness—Hamlet's indecision is the standard example—and our imaginations will correct that weakness on their own; convincingly, moreover, for we graft the missing virtue onto a character whose imperfection makes him believable. The same principles apply when we try (as here) to describe human wholeness not concretely as the artist does, but abstractly: we are on firmest ground when we state the case negatively. To cite an historical instance, the Buddha's characterization of enlightenment as the absence of hatred, greed, and ignorance draws its force from being solidly anchored in real life: its key terms refer to traits we live with all the time. But if we try to restate his formula in positive terms and say that to be enlightened is to be filled with love, wisdom, and an impartial acceptance of everything, our description becomes abstract. Obviously we have some acquaintance with these virtues, but acquaintance is not what is at stake. The goal is to be suffused with these virtues; to be filled by them completely. That we have only the faintest notion of what these positive terms mean when they are raised to their maximum, goes without saying.

DEFINITION OF A JIVAMUKTI

So now we have two wise caveats before us: Darwin's, that we don't know what the *summum bonum* is; and Buddha's, that we do best to approach it negatively. I propose to throw these warnings to the wind and attempt a positive depiction of a *jivamukti*, as the Indians would refer to a fully realized person: a *jiva* (soul) that is *mukti* (liberated, enlightened) in this very life. The project must fail, of course, but that doesn't keep it from being interesting. Perhaps, in keeping with the tragic flaw theory I just alluded to, its very failure may induce the reader to round out in his own imaging the picture which words can never adequately portray.

An enlightened being, I am proposing, is one who is in touch with his deepest unconscious, an unconscious which (for reasons I shall be introducing) deserves to be considered sacred. Our century has acquainted us with regions of our minds that are hidden from us and the powerful ways they control our perceptions. My thesis is that underlying these proximate layers of our unconscious minds is a final substrate that opens mysteriously onto the world as it actually is. To have access to this final substrate is to be objective in the best sense of the word and to possess the virtues and benefits that go with this objectivity.

Normally we are not in touch with this objective component of ourselves—which paradoxically is also our deepest subjective component—because intermediate layers of our unconscious screen it from us while at the same time screening the bulk of the world from us. Our interests, drives, and concerns, their roots largely hidden from our gaze, cause us to see what we want to see and need to see; most of the rest of reality simply passes us by. The Tibetans make this point by saying that when a pickpocket meets a saint, what he sees are his pockets. Moreover, the things we do see we see through lenses that are "prescription ground," so to speak; our interests and conditionings distort the way they appear to us. When poor children are asked to draw a penny they draw it larger than do children for whom pennies are commonplace; it looms larger in their minds' eye. In many such ways, what we take to be objective facts are largely psychological constructs, as the Latin *factum*, "that which is made," reminds us.

This much is now psychological truism. We enter more interesting terrain when we note that at a deeper level the thoughts and feelings that control what we see are themselves shaped by what the Buddha called *the three poisons:* desire (lust, greed, grasping), aversion (fear, hatred, anger), and ignorance.[a] And the greatest of these is ignorance. For it is ignorance—most pointedly ignorance concerning our true identity, who we really are—that causes us to divide the world into what we like and dislike. Thinking that we are separate selves,[b] we seek what augments these selves and shun what threatens them. What we call our "self" is the amalgam of desires and aversions that we have wrapped tightly, like the elastic of a golf ball, around the core of separate identity that is its center.

This tight, constricted, golf-ball self is inevitably in for hard knocks, but what concerns us here is that on average it doesn't feel very good. Anxiety hovers 'round its edges. It can feel victimized

---

[a] I could get where I want to go through any of the great traditions, but having started with Buddhism, I shall continue with it where historical pointers seem helpful.

[b] One of the most interesting and original recent analyses of this most universal (yet ultimately questionable) assumption is to be found in Alex Comfort's *I and That* (New York: Crown Publishers, 1979). Many studies now approach this subject in terms of both Asian and Western thought, but few (in addition) draw recent science as ably into the discussion as does this one.

and grow embittered. It is easily disappointed and can become unstrung. To others it often seems no prettier than it feels to itself: petty, self-centered, drab, and bored.

I am deliberately putting down this golf-ball self—hurling it to the ground, as it were, to see how high our total self can bounce; how far toward heaven it can rise. To rise, it must break out of the hard rubber strings that are normally stretched so tightly around it, encasing it in what Alan Watts called "the skin-encapsulated ego." If we change our image from rubber to glass and picture the three poisons as a lens that refracts light waves in keeping with our private, importunate demands, then release from such egocentric distortions will come through progressively decreasing our lenses' curve—reducing their bulge. The logical terminus of this would then be clear glass. Through this glass we would be able to see things objectively, as they are in themselves in their own right.

This clear glass, which for purposes of vision is equivalent to no glass at all, is our sacred unconscious. It is helpful to think of it as an absence because, like window glass, it functions best when it calls no attention to itself. But it is precisely its absence that makes the world available to us: "the less there is of self, the more there is of Self," as Eckhart put the matter. From clear glass we have moved to no glass—the removal of everything that might separate subject from object, self from world. Zennists use the image of the Great Round Mirror. When the three poisons are removed from it, it reflects the world just as it is.

To claim that human consciousness can move permanently into this condition may be going too far, but advances along the asymptotic curve that slopes in its direction are clearly perceptible. When our aversion lens is powerful, bulging toward the limits of a semicircle, we like very little that comes our way. The same holds, of course, for our desire lens which is only the convex side of our aversion's concave: the more these bend our evaluations toward our own self-interests the less we are able to appreciate things in their own right. Blake's formulation of the alternative to this self-centered outlook has become classic. "If the doors of perception were cleansed everything would appear to man as it is, infinite."

The fully realized human being is one whose doors of perception have been cleansed. And these doors, which up to this point I have referred to as windows, I am here envisioning as successive layers of our unconscious minds. Those that are near the surface vary from person to person for they are deposited by our idiosyncratic childhood experiences. At some level, though, we encounter the three poisons (once again, desire, aversion, and ignorance) that are common to mankind and perhaps in some degree essential for our human functioning. But the deepest layer, we have seen, is really a no-layer, for being a glass door ajar, or a mirror that discloses things other than itself, it isn't there. Even if it were there, in what sense could we call it ours? For when we look toward it we see simply—world.

This opening out onto the world's infinity is one good reason for calling this deepest stratum of the human unconscious sacred, for surely holiness has something to do with the whole. But the concreteness of Blake's formulation is instructive. He doesn't tell us that a cleansed perception discloses the Infinite per se. It finds it in the things at hand, in keeping with those Buddhist stories which tell us that the most sacred scriptures are its unwritten pages—an old pine tree gnarled by wind and weather or a skein of geese flying across the autumn sky.

DESCRIPTION OF A JIVAMUKTI

Thus far I have defined a *jivamukti;* it remains to describe him or her. What does life feel like to such a person, and how does s-he appear to others.

Basically s-he lives in the unvarying presence of the numinous. This does not mean that s-he is excited or "hyped"; his/her condition has nothing to do with adrenalin flow, or with manic states that call for depressive ones to balance the emotional account. It's more like what Kipling had in mind when he said of one of his characters, "He believed that all things were one big miracle, and when a man knows that much he knows something to go upon." The opposite of the sense of the sacred is not serenity or sobriety. It is drabness; taken-for-grantedness. Lack of interest. The humdrum and prosaic.

All other attributes of a *jivamukti* must be relativized against this one absolute: his/her honed sense of the astounding mystery of everything.[1] All else we say of him must have a yes/no quality. Is s-he always happy? Well, yes and no. On one level s-he emphatically is not; if s-he were s-he couldn't "weep with those who mourn"—s-he would be an unfeeling monster, a callous brute. If anything, a realized soul is *more* in touch with the grief and sorrow that is part and parcel of the human condition, knowing that it, too, needs to be accepted and lived as all life needs to be lived. To reject the shadow side of life, to pass it by with averted eyes refusing our share of common sorrow while expecting our share of common joy would cause the unlived, rejected shadows to deepen in us as fear of death. A story that is told of the recent Zen Master Shaku Soen points up the dialectical stance of the realized soul toward the happiness we are noting. When he was able to do so, he liked to take an evening stroll through a nearby village. One evening he heard wailing in a house he was passing and, on entering quietly, found that the householder had died and his family and neighbors were crying. Immediately he sat down and began crying too. An elderly gentleman, shaken by this display of emotion in a famous master, remarked, "I would have thought that you at least were beyond such things." "But it is this which puts me beyond it," the Master replied through his sobs.[2]

The Master's tears we can understand; the sense in which he was "beyond" them is more difficult to fathom, like the peace that passeth understanding. The peace that comes when a man is hungry and finds food, is sick and recovers, or is lonely and finds a friend— peace of this sort is readily intelligible. But the peace that passeth understanding comes when the pain of life is not relieved. It shimmers on the crest of a wave of pain; it is the spear of frustration transformed into a shaft of light. The Master's sobs were real, yet paradoxically they did not erode the yes-experience of the East's "it is as it should be" and the West's "Thy will be done."

In our efforts to conceive the human best, everything turns on an affirmation that steers between cynicism on the one hand and sentimentality on the other. A realized self isn't incessantly, and thereby oppressively, cheerful—oppressively, not only because we suspect some pretense in his unvarying smile, but because it underscores our moodiness by contrast. Not every room a *jivamukti* enters floods with sunlight; he can flash indignation and upset money changers' tables. Not invariance but appropriateness is his hallmark, an appropriateness that has the whole repertoire of emotions at its command. The Catholic Church is right in linking radiance with sanctity, but the paradoxical, "in spite of" character of this radiance must again be stressed. Along with being a gift to be received, life is a task to be performed. The adept performs it: whatever his hand finds to do, he does with all his might. Even if it proves his lot to walk stretches of life as a desert waste, he *walks* them rather than pining for alternatives. Happiness enters as by-product. What matters focally, as the Zen Master Dogen never tired of noting, is resolved.

If a *jivamukti* isn't forever radiating sweetness and light, neither does he constantly emit blasts of energy. He can be forceful when need be; we find it restoring rather than draining to be in his presence, and he has reserves to draw on, as when Socrates stood all night in trance and outpaced the militia with bare feet on ice. In general, though, we sense him/her as relaxed and composed rather than charged—the model of the dynamic and magnetic personality tends to have a lot of ego in it; it demands attention. Remember, everything save the adept's access to inner vistas, the realms of gold I am calling the sacred unconscious, must be relativized. If leadership is called for the adept steps forward, otherwise he is just as happy to follow. He isn't debarred from being a guru, but equally he does not need to be one—he doesn't need disciples to prop up his ego. Focus or periphery, limelight or shadow, it doesn't really matter. Both have their opportunities, both their limitations.

All these relativities I have mentioned—happiness, energy, prominence, impact—pertain to the *jivamukti's* finite self which he progressively pushes aside as he makes his way toward his final, sacred unconscious. As his goal is an impersonal, impartial one, his identification with it involves a dying to his finite selfhood. This finite self is engaged in a vanishing act, as Coomaraswamy suggested when he wrote, "Blessed is the man on whose tomb can be written, *Hic jacet nemo*—"here lies no one."

But having insisted above that there is only one absolute or constant in the journey toward this self-naughting; namely, the sense of the sacred, that luminous mystery in which all things are bathed, I must now admit that there is another: the realization of how far we all are from the goal that beckons, how many ranges of hills remain to be crossed. "Why callest thou me good? . . . " As human beings we are made to surpass ourselves and are truly ourselves only when transcending ourselves. Only the slightest of barriers separates us from our sacred unconscious; it is infinitely close to us. But we are infinitely far from it, so for us the barrier looms as a mountain that we must remove with our own hands. We scrape away at the earth, but in vain; the mountain remains. Still we go on digging at the mountain, in the name of God or whatever. For the most part we only hear of the final truth; very rarely do we actually see it. The mountain isn't there. It never was there.

NOTES

1. Isaac Newton provides a lovely instance of the quality I am thinking of. What could be more everyday or obvious than gravity, enabling and ruling (as it does) our every action. Yet Newton pierced through our habituation with the force to see that it is incomprehensible. "That one body may act upon another at a distance through a vacuum without the mediation of anything else," he wrote to a friend, "is to me so great an absurdity that . . . no man who has in philosophic matters a competent faculty of thinking could ever fall into it." Quoted in Gary Zukav, *The Dancing Wu Li Masters* (New York: William Morrow, 1979), p. 49.

2. Irmgard Schloegel, *The Wisdom of the Zen Masters* (New York: New Directions, 1975), p. 21.

·11·

THE INCREDIBLE ASSUMPTION*

This final selection involves a change of pace. Its different style derives from its having been delivered as a sermon in Rockefeller Chapel of the University of Chicago in 1960. It is thus the earliest of the writings here assembled; but as its thesis pervades them all, it draws them together and rounds them off as a finale.

One hears on all sides that the conflict between science and religion is over. For four centuries the battle has raged: in astronomy over the earth's position in the universe; in geology over the earth's age; in biology over the evolutionary hypothesis; in psychology over Freud's right to "peep and botanize into man's soul." Bitter the struggle has been, and long. Yet (so runs the tale) it has achieved its purpose. Resolution has been secured, concord established. Councils of bishops now speak of scientists as having a religious obligation to follow the truth wherever it leads, and scientists, rejecting the Comptean thesis that religion is to be superseded by science, are busy setting up institutes for religion in an age of science. Occasionally a bible-belt college shows bad form by refusing to allow evolution to be taught, or a Jesuit priest writes an eyebrow-raising book on the phenomenon of man. But these are exceptions. Concord and good fellowship are the orders of the day. For is truth not one, and are not science and religion but two complementary approaches to it?

In the midst of so much agreement, a demur may prove refreshing. Several years devoted to teaching religion at one of the leading

* Reprinted with negligible changes from *The Pulpit* 32, no. 2 (February 1961).

scientific institutions of our day has led me to see the matter in a somewhat different light.

It's true, of course, that the former battles are drawing to a close. Copernicus, Darwin, Freud—geology and Genesis are not today the war cries they used to be.[1] But the fact that certain battles have run their course is no guarantee that a general armistice has been signed, let alone that a just and durable peace has been established. I, for one, suspect that we are still a long way from the day when lion and lamb shall lie down together, and sages sit, each under his own disciplinary vine and fig tree, in full accord.

As I shall be saying some things about science in the minutes ahead, it is important that I interject a disclaimer. The fact that I happen to be in the employ of an institution polarized around science should be taken to mean no more than just that. A British statesman once confessed that his knowledge of mathematics stopped with a desperate finality just where the difficulties began. I could easily paraphrase that statement in present context; a college major in any of the sciences could step to the board and produce equations that would bring my thinking to instant halt. Still, it is impossible to teach at a place like M.I.T. without encountering certain winds of doctrine, and over the years a vision of the program on which science is embarked has come to take shape in my mind.

It has six parts.

First, we shall create life. In a rudimentary way—with the giant molecules, amino acids, and viruses—we have achieved this breakthrough already.

Second, we shall create minds. At this point some of us are likely to suspect a giant finesse,[2] but no matter: cybernetics, univacs, analogue computers—the analogy between minds and thinking machines is being pressed to the hilt.

Third, we shall create adjusted individuals via chemistry: tranquilizers and energizers, barbiturates and amphetamines, a complete pharmacopeia to control our moods and feelings.

Fourth, we shall create the good society via "behavioral engineering," a program of conditioning, liminal and subliminal, which through propaganda and hidden persuaders will induce men to behave in ways conducive to the commonweal.

Fifth, we shall create religious experiences by way of the psychedelics: LSD, mescalin, psilocybin, and their kin.

Sixth, we shall conquer death; achieve physical immortality by a combination of organ transplants and geriatrics that first arrest the aging process and then roll it back in rejuvenation. (See Robert Ettinger, *The Prospect of Immortality.*)

I hasten to insert two qualifications. I have not heard any scientist list these six objectives as parts of a single program, and there are many who discount all but the first. But the basic point stands. Each of the six parts of this emerging program commands not just the labors but the faith of some of our finest scientists. Several years ago I invited B. F. Skinner, dean of American experimental psychologists, to discuss with my students the behaviorally engineered utopia he had sketched in *Walden Two*. In introducing him I said that I wanted the students to have major purchase on his time, but I wanted to ask one question and I would ask it at the start. A decade had passed since he wrote that book; had his thinking changed significantly in the interval? Frankly I expected him to enter some qualifications, to confess that he had been a somewhat younger man then and that things were proving to be a bit more complicated than he had supposed. To my surprise his answer was the opposite. "My thoughts certainly have changed," he said. "This thing is coming faster than I had suspected would be possible."

Perhaps my theology has been inadequately demythologized, but I have difficulty squaring this sixfold program with religion. To the extent that it is taken seriously, God would seem indeed to be dead; to the extent that it is actualized, he will be buried. Instead of a thing of the past, the conflict between science and religion may be shaping up in proportions greater than any we have thus far known.

I have no wish, however, to pursue this prospect further this morning. Instead I should like to reverse the drift I have followed up to this point. Having refused to cry peace where there is no peace, let me now ask whether science, whatever the conscious stance of its practitioners, does not in fact provide us with some clues as to what religion is essentially about.

What is the upshot of man's venture into reality by way of science? Brush aside the details of specific discoveries that are being reported at the rate of two million a year and come at once to the point. From the theoretical standpoint the basic upshot of science is that it has disclosed a universe which in its factual nature is infinitely beyond anything we could have imagined while relying on our unaided senses.

A routine recall of two or three well-known facts will make this abundantly evident. Light travels at the rate of 186,000 miles per second. That's about seven times around the world. Now take the time-span that separates us from Christ and multiply it, not fifty times, but fifty thousand times, and you have the approximate time it takes a beam of light to move from one end of our galaxy to the other.

Our sun rotates around the center of our galaxy at a speed of one hundred sixty miles per second. That's fast; how fast we can perhaps appreciate if we recall the difficulty we have had getting rockets to attain a speed of seven miles per second, the speed required for them to escape from our earth's atmosphere. The sun travels roughly twenty-two times as fast as this escape rate, at which speed it takes it approximately 224 million years to complete one revolution around our galaxy. If these figures sound astronomical, we must remember that they are actually parochial, for they are confined to our own galaxy. Andromeda, our second closest neighbor, is one-and-a-half million light-years removed, beyond which the universe falls away abysmally, range after range, world after world, island universe after island universe. In other directions the figures are equally incomprehensible. Avogadro's number tells us that the number of molecules in four-and-a-half drams of water (roughly half an ounce) is 6.023 times 10^{23}, roughly 100,000 billion billion. It's enough to make one dizzy; enough to make the mind reel, and spin, and cry out for a stop. Nay more. From the vantage of our ordinary senses the vision is incredible—utterly, absolutely, completely incredible.

Only, of course, it's true.

Now along comes an Isaiah, a Christ, a Paul, a Saint Francis, a Buddha; along come men who are religiously the counterparts of Copernicus, Newton, Faraday, Kepler, and they tell us something equally incredible about the universe in its value dimension. They tell us of depth upon depth of value falling away from this visible world and our ordinary perceptions. They tell us that this universe in all its vastness is permeated to its very core by love. And that's incredible. I look at the newspaper every morning and say to myself, "It cannot be!" Yet in my reflective moments I find myself adding, "Is it, after all, any more incredible—does it any more exceed the limits of our normal human experience—than what my science colleagues are saying in their sphere?"

Of course the scientists have the advantage here, for they can prove their hypotheses whereas values and meanings elude the devices of science like the sea slips through the nets of fishermen. But this only leads me to press the analogy between science and religion farther. The factual marvels of the physical universe are not evident to the naked eye. Who, relying only on his own gross, unaided vision, could suspect that electrons are circling their nuclei at the rate of a million million times a second? Such truths are disclosed to the scientists only through certain key perceptions, certain crucial experiments. The far-flung embroideries of science and the scientific world view are really based on a relatively small number of such experiments.

If this be true in science, why not in religion as well? If factual truth is disclosed not through routine perceptions but through key or crucial ones, might not this be the case with religious truth as well? The Lord appearing high and lifted up to Isaiah; the heavens opening to Christ at his baptism; the universe turning into a bouquet of flowers for Buddha beneath the Bo tree. John reporting, "I was on an island called Patmos, and I was in a trance." Saul struck blind on the Damascus road. For Augustine it was the voice of a child saying, "Take, read"; for Saint Francis a voice which seemed to come from the crucifix. It was while Saint Ignatius sat by a stream and watched the running water and that curious old cobbler Jacob Boehme was looking at a pewter dish that there came to each that news of another world which it is always religion's business to convey.

A final step in the comparison is needed. If the universe of science is not evident to our ordinary senses but is elaborated from certain key perceptions, it is equally the case that these perceptions require their appropriate instruments: microscopes, Palomar telescopes, cloud chambers, and the like. Again, is there any reason why the same should not hold for religion? A few words by that late, shrewd lay theologian, Aldous Huxley, make the point well. "It is a fact, confirmed and reconfirmed by two or three thousand years of religious history," he wrote, "that Ultimate Reality is not clearly and immediately apprehended except by those who have made themselves loving, pure in heart, and poor in spirit." Perhaps such purity of heart is the indispensable instrument for disclosing the key perceptions on which religion's incredible assumption is grounded.

With the unaided eye a small faint smudge can be detected in the constellation of Orion and doubtless an imposing cosmological theory founded on this smudge. But no amount of theorizing, however ingenious, could ever tell us as much about the galactic and extragalactic nebulae as can direct acquaintance by means of a good telescope, camera, and spectrascope.

I don't know in what direction such thoughts drive your mind; mine they drive in the direction of God. But the word doesn't matter; it's the assumption itself that counts, or rather the reality to which it points. Just as science has found the power of the sun itself to be locked in the atom, so religion (by whatsoever name) proclaims the glory of the eternal to be reflected in the simplest elements of time: a leaf, a door, an unturned stone. And so, for this quasi-religious, quasi-secular age, these lines titled "White Heron" by John Ciardi:

> *What lifts the heron leaning on the air*
> *I praise without a name. A crouch, a flare,*
> *a long stroke through the cumulus of trees,*
> *a shaped thought at the sky—then gone. O rare!*
> *Saint Francis, being happiest on his knees,*
> *would have cried Father! Cry anything you please*
>
> *But praise. By any name or none. But praise*
> *the white original burst that lights*
> *the heron on his two soft kissing kites.*
> *When saints praise heaven lit by doves and rays,*
> *I sit by pond scums till the air recites*
> *Its heron back. And doubt all else. But praise.*[3]

NOTES

1. In 1960 the Creationists were not yet visible on the national scene.

2. See my "Human versus Artificial Intelligence," in John Roslansky, ed., *The Human Mind* (Amsterdam: North Holland Publishing Co., 1967).

3. John Ciardi, "The White Heron," in *I Marry You* (New Brunswick, N.J.: Rutgers University Press, 1958). Used by permission of the author.

INDEX